Anonymous

Newport and the resorts of Narragansett Bay, 1878,

Containing maps of Newport and Narragansett Bay, yacht lists, tide tables,

list of Newport summer residents, etc., etc

Anonymous

Newport and the resorts of Narragansett Bay, 1878,
Containing maps of Newport and Narragansett Bay, yacht lists, tide tables, list of Newport summer residents, etc., etc

ISBN/EAN: 9783337733667

Printed in Europe, USA, Canada, Australia, Japan

Cover: Foto ©ninafisch / pixelio.de

More available books at **www.hansebooks.com**

NEWPORT,

AND THE

RESORTS OF NARRAGANSETT BAY, 1878.

CONTAINING

MAPS OF NEWPORT AND NARRAGANSETT BAY, YACHT
LISTS, TIDE TABLES,

LIST OF NEWPORT SUMMER RESIDENTS,

ETC., ETC.

———◆———

Published by Wm. P. Clarke.

Chapter 1.

NARRAGANSETT BAY.

NARRAGANSETT BAY is a beautiful sheet of water extending from Point Judith and Seaconnet Point on the south, to Bullock's Point, six miles below Providence, on the north, being about twenty-eight miles long, and varying in width from three to twelve miles.

Besides being the great thoroughfare for commerce, it abounds in resorts that attract the eye, then the heart and leave their impression there forever. Here nature has lavished her treasures with a prodigal hand. From its earliest discovery it has borne the name of the "Paradise of the Western World"—and well does it deserve the name. Her bosom is thickly studded with islands, fertile, picturesque and beautiful, around which history and fiction have woven many a romantic legend.

Over these waters the dusky savage paddled his bark canoe ; under the shade of the ancient forests the amorous warrior wooed his dusky bride. Over these waters in later days glided the vessels of every nation on the earth, and the stroke of the white man's axe was heard ringing through the aisles of the forests on her shores. Little by little were the ancient owners of the soil driven out ; little by little did the whites extend their borders, until the savage was driven from the land of his birth, from the graves of his ancestors, from his beautiful island and placid waters, and pushed back by an iron hand towards the setting sun.

With the whites came love and hate, war and peace, wealth and poverty. Over the bosom of the bay that had hitherto been pressed by naught heavier than a birchen canoe, now glided the stern vessel of war, the swift sailing privateer, the peaceful merchantma: and the bold pirate.

Then came the low, black slaver, bringing to shores those miserable beings that were so long el in this great country of *liberty*.

Yes, the shores of this bay are peopled with upon which the Almighty has always delighted to blessings, and prosperity has always followed footsteps. Entering the bay from the westward object that attracts the attention is Point Judith, with its revolving light. This is one of the roughest points on this coast, and fortunate is he who is able to enjoy the surrounding scenery.

Off toward Brenton's Reef, which runs out just off the southwest point of Rhode Island is the light-ship. Brenton's Reef, which, through rain or shine, summer and winter, storm or calm, breasts the waves and throws her light far across the billows, a comfort and guide to the storm-tossed mariner. Directly opposite to the left is Narragansett Pier, a delightful little resort, of which we shall speak hereafter. Directly ahead of you lies Conanicut Island, upon the south point of which stands Beaver Tail Light-House. This island was named after the noted Indian chief, Canonicus, who made his home here. Just off the west shore of the island, about midway of it is Dutch Island, with its light. The harbor there will accommodate a large number of vessels, and is much frequented by storm-bound crafts. Conanicut is developing into quite a popular summer resort, the Dumplings at the south and Conanicut Park at the north end being the principal points of interest. It is said in favor of the park that in that vicinity Captain Kidd, the noted pirate, buried an untold amount of treasure. It is but fair to say that though industriously searched for by past generations, no one ever succeeded in finding it. At the south end they have the Old Fort and the Dumplings. Opposite the Dumplings that point that runs out so abruptly is Brenton's Point, now owned by the government, and occupied by Fort Adams. As you enter the harbor upon the right you have Lime Rocks, the home of Ida Lewis, upon your left Goat Island, or the Torpedo Station as it is called. The island was occupied by a fort in Revolutionary times, called Fort George, latterly by Fort Walcott, and now by a combustible manufactory. This old weather beaten town on your right that looks as if it needed painting is Newport, of which we shall make mention hereafter. Leaving the harbor the first object of interest we meet is the Poor House upon Coaster's Harbor Island. The island was discovered and named by William Brenton and his sons, in the year 1638, while exploring in a boat. The party came from Portsmouth, and were in search of a suitable location for a new town. They landed at Coaster's Harbor, and gave it the name it still retains. Almost west and midway between Coaster's Harbor and Conanicut is Rose Island, with its light. There was once a small earthwork or fort upon the island, a few vestiges of which remain. Directly north, abruptly rising from the water is a fertile and verdant island, known as Gould Island ; it is owned by Commodore Homans, of the New York Yacht Club. He spends his summers in this secluded retreat. We next reach Prudence Island, which is one of the largest in the bay, and is surrounded by a brood of smaller ones, namely : Hope, Patience, Despair, Dyer to the southeast, and Hog further to the eastward, and north of Rhode Island. Hog Island received its name from the fact that the early settlers of Rhode Island sent all their hogs there to prevent them from destroying their crops. About midway between Newport and Providence is Rocky Point, which is situated at the north part of Warwick Neck. This is a most popular resort, and will be more particularly mentioned in another chapter.

On the opposite side of the Neck is another resort, known as Oakland Beach. This has in years past been a popular resort, but the hotel was closed last year, and the place was visited by but a few straggling picnicers.

A little further up the bay is Gaspee Point, where in the year 1772 the Gaspee was burned by the Americans. This vessel was a revenue cruiser, sent to keep an eye upon the King's customs. The commander, whose name was Duddingston, made himself particularly obnoxious by his acts of petty tyranny. At length she started for Providence, but unfortunately got aground. The news soon spread, and while she lay in this helpless condition the people assembled and compelled the crew to surrender, after which they burned the vessel.

Immediately opposite is Bullock's Point; and from thence to Providence there are a number of resorts on either side of the bay. On the east side there is Riverside, Cedar Grove, Silver Spring, Ocean Cottage and Squantum ; upon the west side there are Smith's Palace and Field's Point. All these places will be more particularly mentioned hereafter.

During the early history of this country many stirring events transpired in or near the waters of Narragansett Bay.

Just north of the Island of Aquidneck, or Rhode Island, is Mount Hope Bay. Upon the west side of the bay upon a neck of land now known as Bristol, stands Mount Hope, where King Philip breathed his last, slain by the hand of a traitor. During the Revolutionary War the proud navies of both England and France plowed the waters of this bay, and her shores have often echoed to the thunder of hostile cannon.

At the outbreak of that memorable struggle Captain Wallace, of the sloop-of-war Rose, then stationed at Newport, began a marauding warfare against the inhabitants of the bay, which he carried on nearly two years before driven away. From Conanicut and Rhode Island they took cattle and sheep ; from Hope Island they cut all the timber. A party of his marines landed upon Prudence, where they burnt one house and a barn. In a skirmish that ensued one man was killed, and another wounded on the American side. The enemy's loss was about the same.

When Major Barton effected the capture that made his name immortal, he started from Warwick Neck just

below Rocky Point, and took his course between Hope
and Prudence Islands. Some of the most important
operations of the war took place in Rhode Island, and
the inhabitants of all the islands we have mentioned as
well as the whole State were of the most patriotic order,
and exerted themselves to the utmost to aid in prose-
cuting the War for Independence.

But scenes of peace followed those of war, and the
shores and islands of the bay again resounded to the
echo of busy labor and toil. Instead of grim ships of
war, Her waters are now plowed by the busy merchant-
man, the puffy, wheezy tug and lumberly barge, the graceful schooner and the smoky propellor constantly bringing
to all her shores untold wealth, and carrying to other
markets the products of her skill. During the summer
season she is transformed into a race track, and on
almost every pleasant day you may see the graceful
yachts flying along under a cloud of canvas for the
amusement of the many who visit these waters. Nature
has also lent her aid in making the visits popular to the
lover of sport, and to the angler, for no where can such
fish be found as lurk in many a dark hole, known only
to some old fisherman who will gladly take you out for
a day. And when it comes to clam-bakes, where in this
wide world can such clams be found? Were I a poet I
would insert here a glowing poem to the clam, but as I
am not, we leave it for those who shall sample them at
Squantum and Rocky Point this Summer.

Newport.

Chapter 2.

NEWPORT-OLD AND NEW-SETTLEMENT-PROG-
RESS—WAR—DECAY—SECOND GROWTH.

E are well aware that to the tourist and pleasure seeker facts and dates, and history are dry
reading. But the Newport of the present is
so inseparably linked with the Newport of the
past, that the additional charm lent to the many historical spots will well repay for the trouble of a few dates.

Perhaps no place in our country has suffered so many
reverses and passed through so many vicissitudes of for-
tune as Newport.

From being the asylum of outcasts, she, with rapid
strides, placed herself in the foremost ranks of American cities ; and from the ashes of British devastation
she has risen, phœnix like—if not to her former position
among mercantile cities — among watering places,
" Queen of the Seas."

November 2d, 1637, William Coddington and fifteen
others were disarmed for dissenting from certain judg-
ments of the General Court of Massachusetts. In the
May following the same court notified some twelve of
them "that they had license to leave the Colony."

These men set out and finally landed at Pocasset—
now Portsmouth—on the then Island of Aquidneck.

Through the kindly efforts of Roger Williams, who had already settled at Providence, they obtained the deed of the island from the Indians, for the consideration of " forty fathom of white beads."

In the spring of 1639 Mr. Coddington and seventeen others left Portsmouth and settled in Newport. The first settlers of the island, were, as we have seen, the " exiled of exiles."

The bigotry and intolerance of the old world ecclesias tics had driven the Puritans to our shores, and failing to learn from their own miseries the lesson of toleration, they in turn drove the "Freethinkers" from their own midst. The exiles being men of culture and piety, laid deep the foundations for that cultivation and that love of civil and religious liberty for which the State has ever been noted.

From this period until the War for Independence, Newport's history was one of continued progress.

As early as 1640 one Robert Lenthall was engaged to teach a public school, " the first in America, and probably the first supported by public charge in the world.

From that early beginning has grown one of the finest school systems of our country.

The delightful climate, fertile soil and a remarkably brilliant green verdure soon attracted the population from less favored spots, and Newport rapidly became the most considerable town of the new colonies.

As early as 1656 the Quakers had, driven by the inhospitable reception given them by the other colonies, found their way to the " Isle of Peace." They have left a decided imprint upon the character of the place, and to this day their June Meeting is one of *the* events in the life of Newport.

In 1644 the island then known as Aquidneck was ordered by the General Court of Election to be called Rhode Island, a name derived from "Roode Eiland," a name given to the channels in 1614 by Adriaen Block, a Dutch navigator. Although there is another and more popular theory that it was named after its resemblance to the Isle of Rhodes in the Mediterranean Sea.

As early as 1728 Dean Berkeley had pronounced Newport "the most thriving place in the new country." In 1730 the population had reached the sum of four thousand six hundred and forty, or seven hundred more than that of Providence. During the year 1763 five hundred and thirty-four vessels cleared from this port, employing the grand aggregate of two thousand two hundred sailors. Two hundred of these vessels were employed in foreign traffic, and regular packets plied between this port and London.

New Yorkers were condolingly informed "that with their natural facilities they might in time become a formidable rival in trade and commerce were they to possess themselves of an energy and enterprise equal to that of the Newporters." Newport merchants rapidly became opulent, their homes were elegant with "curious carvings, wainscoted walls, tiled fire-places and grand old staircases."

Newport merchants themselves occupied the heights, and the cliffs, and the shores with their own magnificent residences, instead of as now giving up all her grand sites to the wealthy of other cities.

Newporters were among the first to resist British authority ; none fought more tenaciously ; none suffered more severely.

According to one authority the fort at Newport had fired upon the King's ship Squirrel, in the year 1764.

The guns of Concord and Lexington found the material in readiness, and at their first flash one thousand men trained under such daring leaders as the privateersmen Dennis and Read, sprang to arms. They had been trained to hardships, and played no unimportant part in the struggle for independence. December 6th, 1776, the British under General Clinton took possession of the Town and island, and occupied them nearly three years. The command was relinquished by General Clinton to Earl Percy the following January, and he in turn gave it over to General Prescott in May of the same year. Prescott was afterwards captured by Colonel Barton at the Overing House.

The story of his capture is briefly this: General Prescott had made his headquarters some four miles out of Newport, in a lovely situation not far from Lawton's valley. They were over a mile from the body of the troops, and protected only by a sentry and a guard-ship lying in the bay. Colonel Barton conceived the idea of taking the British General, and taking two whale-boats manned with picked crews, on the evening of July 9th, 1777, he ran into Redwood Creek, and disarming the sentry took both sentry and commander prisoner, and passing under the shadow of the guard-ship reached the American camp in safety.

The Revolution left Newport and the Island desolate and in ruins.

The magnificent forests that had graced the Island were destroyed ; stores, homes and farms were pillaged ; fences destroyed, walls razed, and the public records carried off and sunk in the waters of Hell Gate. Over four hundred buildings were destroyed, none of any importance being left in a tenantable condition, save only Trinity Church, which, as the theory is, was left through regard for the crown that to this day caps its spire.

A French writer in speaking of Newport says :

"Since the peace everything is changed, the reign of solitude is only interrupted by groups of idle men standing with folded arms at the corner of streets, houses falling to ruin, miserable shops which present nothing but a few coarse stuffs, * * * * grass growing in the public square in front of the Court of Justice, rags stuffed in the windows, * * * * * everything announces misery." But he adds further on in the dismal narrative, " the Rhode Islander does not beg, and he does not steal.

Such was the rise and fall of Newport.

The New is indeed changed—in summer. The Newport of to-day is a combination of the old and the new. The winter life could fittingly be described by the Frenchman's words just quoted. After the "season" is over the streets are lined and the corners are grouped with loafing men. They shift only with the sun, rise when it rises, retire when it sets. They stand and look at the sky, then at the earth, then at one another. Then they blink, and yawn, and doze, from sunrise till noon-tide, from noon-tide till sunset ; until as Colonel Higginson says in his "Oldport Days," the authorities have been compelled to take down the hitching-posts, and the telegraph poles have been condemned because of loafers congregating around them and blockading the streets.

But the Newport of to-day that is presented to the visiting stranger is not the Newport of winter, but the lively, dashing and rich watering place. It has always been the centre of American culture, and has now become the summer centre of her wealth and fashion.

Before our late civil war the hotel life of Newport was considerable, and great numbers of Southerners flocked here to escape the extreme heat of their own homes. Since then very few Southerners have made the place a resort, and hotels have given place to palatial residences and airy cottages, unrivalled by those of any watering place, many of them costing from twenty to five hundred thousand dollars.

All of the Newport of to-day that renders it famous is clustered on the avenue, the cliffs and the beach. Here millions of dollars of the wealth of New York, Boston, Philadelphia, Baltimore and Chicago have been invested.

In summer a new life is infused into the quiet old seaport town. Thames street is crowded with teams until it becomes a second Broadway. Bellevue Avenue, between the hours of five and seven P. M., presents one of the gayest scenes imaginable. The horn is heard behind you; you turn—Polo is just over, and down the avenue at a break-neck speed comes the coaching club—five magnificent turn-outs, all four-in-hands—the veritable coaches of olden times of "Merrie England."

At their sides, behind them, in front of them to the length of the avenue in either direction, drawn by

15

thorough-bred horses—tandems, prancing teams, four
and six-in-hands—are barouches, coupes, dog-carts, lan-
daus, cabriolets, and every form of vehicle known and
unknown—all are pressed into the service and lend a
charm to the whirl of life.

Hotel life is only a minor, home life—and the most of
them are palatial homes—the leading feature. Accompanying this feature we find the society aristocratic and
exclusive.

At Newport mornings are the most attractive part of
the day. Guests rise early, and morning shopping, noon
bathing, fashionable dinners and entertainments at the
villas, and balls and promenades at the Ocean House
consume the days in rapid succession.

Chapter 3.

NEWPORT A WATERING PLACE.

CLIMATE AND SCENERY — HARBOR — BEACH — CLIFFS—FORTY STEPS—BOAT HOUSE—SPOUTING CAVE—CASTLE HILL—FORT ADAMS—PURGATORY — HANGING ROCK — WHITEHALL—SACHUEST POINT—INDIAN AVENUE.

NATURE has done all that possibly could be asked to render Newport popular as a watering place. She has given of her stores most lavishly. She has bestowed rugged coasts, with their giant walls; a magnificent beach, safe and smooth, yet having a grand surf; and a harbor in which the largest vessels can ride. She has given coves and ponds, and brooks; and on land valleys, and promontories, and glens. The city itself is built on a beautiful hill, sloping gently to the west, from whose summit a fine view of land and sea is obtained; away to the south the restless ocean stretches, whitened with the sail of every clime; to the north lies the beautiful Narrgansett dotted with numerous islands and enlivened by steamers plying from shore to shore, while to the east and west are seen respectively the hills of Massachusetts and Connecticut. The island within its fifty miles of shore contains a panorama of varied and beautiful scenery. While you may soon weary of the dust and confusion of many watering places relieved only by the presence of some celebrity, and perhaps a fine beach, one can never tire of the beauties and glories of Newport. Whether you visit the cliffs or the shores, or linger around historical spots, you are sure to return again. At each visit her scenery grows wilder and more enchanting, until unconsciously you find yourself walking the same paths, looking at the same scenes time upon time, admiring and wondering with an admiration and wonder that know no abatement, and you reluctantly leave, murmuring—" the Italy of America."

The climate, too, is most salutary. The heat of the most torrid summer is modified by the cool and refreshing breeze from off the ocean, and the most rigid winter is tempered by the gentle influence of the gulf stream that flows near by.

Newport Harbor is one of the finest in our country, and although commerce has left it almost deserted, save only by fishing boats and pleasure yachts, yet in days gone by the merchant vessels of every nationality have sought its crowded wharves, and from its quiet retreat hardy sailors have set sail for lives of adventure.

Approaching Newport from the sea, having left Block Island and Point Judith behind, we pass Brenton's Reef Light-Ship, one of those faithful monitors which along our coast warn the mariner of dangerous shoals. Just ahead of us Beaver Tail Light, on Conanicut Island, sends a greeting. To the right is Fort Adams, with the old "flag still there." To the left is Fort Brown, the round fort on the Dumplings, the sight of which carries us back to Revolutionary times. In the meantime we have passed by Fort Adams, and here to our right, just on the southern end of the inner harbor, lie Lime Rocks, with their friendly light.

The Lime Rocks have been rendered famous by the splendid achievements and heroism of Ida Lewis, the Grace Darling of America.

While our noble steamer is making her way to the landing, dodging the fishing-smacks that persistently anchor in the channel, we will listen to the story of the high daring of the heroine of the Lime Rocks Light.

In these times when examples of Spartan bravery are so few, the world applauds physical daring and courage, no matter by whom it may chance to be exhibited ; but when deeds are accomplished by a woman that would have caused the stoutest heart to quail in their performance, the general enthusiasm knows no bounds. And such has been the experience of this daring character. In 1858, when only sixteen years of age, she put off alone and rescued four men who had been capsized, and who but for the timely aid of our heroine must have perished. In the winter of 1866 she saved the life of a soldier from Fort Adams. Again the same season two men attempting to rescue a sheep from the icy waters of the bay into which it had leaped, were themselves swamped, and their lives were added to the growing list rescued by Ida Lewis.

But a few days after this she rescued a man from the small rock lying between the Lime Rock and shore, over which the water flows at high tide. The man had remained clinging to the wreck of his boat all through the terrible cold of a winter night, and when rescued the water was just closing over him as the tide washed him from his precarious station.

In March, 1869, she performed her most dangerous and noted act of bravery. The weather had been stormy, and at the time of the rescue the waters of the harbor were lashed into a fury. Two soldiers foolishly sought to fight their way through the waves to the Fort in a row-boat. They were soon capsized, and, clinging to their skiff, must soon have drifted out to sea. Being discovered by Mrs. Lewis her cry brought Ida to the rescue. In a moment she was in her boat ; the battle with wind and wave was a most terrible one. Wave after wave dashed over the boat, the spray with its blinding fury was driven by each gust of wind full in her face, and but for a steady nerve the battle must have been a losing one. At last she reached the almost lifeless men, and with the aid of her younger brother drew them into the boat and returned with them to her home.

This last act brought her before the world. Thousands have visited her at her lonely home on the Rocks. Thousands who have not visited her have showered their letters of respect and praise upon her. Others have manifested their regard by more substantial means. The officers and men at Fort Adams made up a purse of over two hundred dollars, which was presented with an appropriate letter from General Hunt. The City of Newport presented her with a beautiful boat, the Rescue, and Jim Fisk built a house for it.

Resolutions were unanimously adopted by the General Assembly of the State of Rhode Island, acknowledging her " valuable services in saving so many lives from drowning." The Life Saving Benevolent Association of New York presented her with a medal and one hundred dollars. The medal bears on one side an engraving representing a wreck and several men standing on the shore near by trying to render assistance.

The reverse shows the motto,

"Vita Felicibus Ausis Servata,"

and, "Presented to Miss Ida Lewis as a testimonial of her skill, courage and humanity, in rescuing two men from drowning in the harbor of Newport, Rhode Island, during a heavy storm on the 29th of March, 1869."

The curious can see Miss Lewis and her medals almost any time at her home on the Rocks.

The long, low island lying just north of the light-house and directly in front of the city is Goat Island, formerly the site of Fort Walcott, whose intrenchments and bomb-proofs are still to be seen. It is now occupied by the U. S. Torpedo Station.

The station is now under command of Captain Breeze and is the only torpedo school in our country. All members of the Naval Academy pass through its course of instruction. It is well supplied with shops and laboratories for carrying on experiments, and its several departments are under the charge of men eminent in their respective branches. All experiments and discoveries are kept secret and access to the island is obtained with difficulty.

Beach and watering place have become so intimately associated by the tourist as to be used almost synonymously, and the first inquiry after having reached Newport is for the beach. Almost any street leading up the hill from Thames street will lead you to Bellevue Avenue. Turning to the right on the avenue Bath road is soon reached and down this road abut one-half a mile lies the beach.

Just back of the beach is Easton's pond, a fresh water body, and further over, across the dam, may be seen the new water works being introduced into the city through the skill and enterprise of Mr. Geo. H. Norman.

The scene from the beach looking seaward is charming. To our right stretch the Cliffs, Newport's most noted walk, reaching far around the south end of the island, presenting their hard, rocky sides to the restless waves. Standing from fifty to sixty feet above low water mark, their slopes masked in splendid succession with the finest villas of modern days, each vieing with its neighbor in the magnificence of its surroundings and the splendor of its own design. To the south, where sea and sky seem to blend in one harmonious shade of blue like floating clouds, are seen the distant sail of some coast-wise ship. Nearer, the white sail of the fishing smack is seen, while the fisherman hauls in his heavily laden net. Far out to the left, bathed with spray and foam by the breaking waves are Easton and Sachuest Points.

The beach with its gay costumes, presents all the colors of the kaleidoscope. From the hours of ten till one the scene is a lively and interesting sight. Hundreds in fantastic costumes are plunging into Neptune's cooling element. The shore is lined with vehicles of every description, their occupants watching the bathers or pleasantly chatting the time away. The beach is extremely safe with very little undertow, so that the most timid may with safety indulge to the fullest extent their longing for a plunge into the surf. Neat bathing-houses line the beach, the use of which can be obtained for fifteen cents, and the like sum will engage a bathing suit should you have been so unfortunate as to have forgotten your own. Busses for the beach will be found at all the boats and trains, and for fifteen cents they will land you at the bathing-houses.

No one who visits Newport should fail to take the Cliff Walk. Certainly no one who stands on the beach and sees down their long line the waves breaking against reef and wall, showering the spray like globules of silver in the sunlight, can resist the temptation.

Although lined with the finest places on the island, the ancient right of fishery is still retained, and their banks are left free to all, and the generosity of the owners of the various estates has provided a fine, broad promenade almost the entire length of this portion of the island. The rock formation is a mingling of a conglomerate and a soft shale, the latter crumbling easily in your hand.

They are also of considerable interest as being the only instance of high, rock-bound, open coast from Maine to Florida.

Just before reaching the beach on Bath Road, turning to the right we enter the Cliff Walk. On our right facing the ocean are the Cliff cottages and hotel. From these a fine view of the island, beach and sea are obtained. While the scene for the entire length of the walk is one to be thoroughly enjoyed, the first spot of special interest is Forty Steps, or Conrad's Cave, at the foot of

Narragansett Avenue. The steps are a favorite resort and one could sit for hours of a pleasant day at their foot watching the heavy swells advancing and retreating, following one another over the rocks in a lazy, sluggish succession. But the genuine lover of the sea will not fail to visit them in a storm. Then far off shore a ponderous wave may be seen, lifting itself higher and higher as it approaches the shore, as though determined to grind to powder the rock that dare oppose it, until, lifting, it throws itself upon the rocks with a plunge, scattering great clouds of spray far up the cliffs. During a storm the whole coast becomes one mass of spray and foam.

The Boat-House is at the southern extremity of the island, just at the foot of Ledge Road. This is a place famous as the resort of fishermen and for clam-bakes. Directly in front is Coggeshall Ledge, forming a natural breakwater and affording an excellent landing. Burton's buss runs within a few rods of the landing and this will be found an excellent starting point for a walk around the cliffs.

Further along we come to Bailey's Beach, and among that mass of rocks piled in wild confusion just across the beach will be found Spouting Rock. Spouting Rock is a cave into which, the wind and tide being favorable, the water rushes with a tremendous velocity, and returning is thrown from fifty to a hundred feet into the air, through an opening in the roof of the cave. A southeast wind and ebbing tide are the requisite conditions. The most enthusiastic lover of nature will be glad to take the avenue for town after a walk around the Cliffs, and while Fort Adams and Castle Hill lie beyond they must be visited when driving. Castle Hill lies, as will be seen by referring to the map, on the extreme western point of the island. The sea view from here is one of the finest on a clear day, Block Island and Point Judith being in sight.

Fort Adams, just at the entrance to the harbor, with the exception of Fortress Monroe, is the largest fort belonging to our government. Although commenced during the administration of President Adams it was not finished until some years later. Fort days—Tuesdays and Fridays—fashionable Newport repairs to the Fort, and the grim old granite walls lose something of their sternness as the crowd clambers over the ramparts or wanders among the galleries. The band plays and for the time all is festivity. The direct route to the Fort is out Thames Street, and via. Wellington and Harrison Avenues. While a very pleasant way is by boat, the sail over and back being very popular.

This for the southern and western portion of the island, and we will turn our attention to the eastern portion, warning the reader that a week or more can easily be devoted to that which we are hurrying so rapidly over.

If we pass across the bathing beach and keep straight up the hill we soon reach the second beach. A short distance from here, and on the cliffs on the west side of the beach is situated Purgatory. This is a chasm one hundred and sixty feet in length ; from eight to fourteen feet wide at the top ; from two to twenty-four feet wide at the bottom, and sixty feet deep. It was probably caused by some violent upheaval of nature,—if closed, the opposite walls would fit the one into the other—although other theories are advanced. Legend has associated the spot with His Satanic Majesty ; and to the north of the place may be seen marks made as he dragged an offending squaw along. And the place where her head lay and the beheading axe chipped the rock can still be seen.

Purgatory Bluffs, as the rocks on the east side of Easton's Point are sometimes called, are as wild and inviting as the cliffs, and before many years the bluffs and the entire point must become popular as a place for summer residences. To the left of Purgatory, looking across the second beach, Hanging Rock, lifted high, faces the sea. Half a mile further on is Whitehall, famous as the home of Berkeley. In this old house, now the property of Yale College, the philosopher waited long years in vain for the twenty thousand pounds promised by Sir Robert Walpole to found his college in the Bermudas. In the shadow of Hanging Rock he wrote "The Minute Philosopher." Berkeley was also the author of the lines :

> " Westward the course of empire takes its way;
>   The four first acts already past,
> A fifth shall close the drama with the day:
>   Time's noblest offspring is the last."

From the second or Sachuest beach, Sachuest Point strikes boldly out to sea. On the east side of this point is the third beach. The southern end of the point is exceedingly rugged, and in the calmest weather its long, broken line of rocks keeps the water in a constant tumult. The fishing near here is excellent and famous.

This beach was the witness of a bold scene in 1778.

The British being in possession of the southern end of the island, and wishing to cut off communication with the north end, had stationed a galley in the passage between the island and the mainland, armed with ten eighteen-pounders and ten swivels. Major Talbot decided to capture her. Taking seventy-five men in a small sloop, on the night of November 4th, he passed the fort and sentinels on land, and favored by darkness and fog ran into and boarded her, and before the British had recovered from their surprise had made all on board prisoners of war.

Indian Avenue has been opened along the third beach and is fast becoming a favorite drive.

Many other places of interest on the island, viz. : the Glen, Lawton's Valley, the Dumplings, and others, have been crowded out of this chapter and will be described in Chapter 6.

Chapter 4.

ANTIQUE NEWPORT.

THAMES STREET — CITY HALL — ARTILLERY
COMPANY—VERNON HOUSE — STATE HOUSE—
ELECTION DAY — JEWISH SYNAGOGUE AND
CEMETERY—OLD MILL—LONG WHARF—GRAV-
ELLY POINT-FORT GREENE—HUNTER HOUSE—
LIBERTY TREE—CHANNING HOUSE—TRINITY
CHURCH—OTHER NOTED PLACES.

" We saw the port.
The strange, old-fashioned, silent town—
The light-house, the dismantled fort,
The wooden houses, quaint and brown."

ISTORY, much of it so remote as to have almost
become a legend, lends a peculiar charm to the
crooked streets and quaint buildings of the older
portion of Newport.

The streets are narrow and cramped, the houses low
studded, gambreled roofed and crumbling. Thames
Street now become the most important business street,
is of itself a curiosity—a relic. It isn't of the nineteenth
century, but of the seventeenth. The narrow, winding
street, lined with dilapidated residences doing service as
stores, carries you back to the days when the Appalachian
range was the limit of the known western world. They

then built after the fashion of England, and not with the
lavish hand òf more modern days. Could 'they speak,
each narrow, winding street, each wharf, crowded with
its ancient, weather-worn buildings, could tell tales
stranger than fiction. Through these streets Washington
and Rochambeau have marched ; in them the clash of
arms has been heard. From these wharves privateers
have set out ; and in their sight many a noble vessel
perished during the struggle of 1778.

In our search for objects of historical interest, we shall
find no better starting place than the Parade. The
Parade is a delta formed by the junction of Broadway
and Thames, and Touro Streets. At the foot of the
Parade—also called Washington Square—on the southwest corner of Thames Street is the City Hall, first built
and used as a granary in 1763, it has since been dignified
by being converted into the headquarters of the city
government. In this building may be seen the escutch-
eon of William Coddington, the first Governor of Rhode
Island.

Just above Thames Street on the south side of the
Square is the Perry House, and further up the hill stands
the house occupied by Commodore Perry after the battle
of Lake Erie. Commodore Perry's fame as the hero of
the battle of Lake Erie is world wide, and in the Island
Cemetery stands a granite shaft erected to his memory
by the State.

Just around the corner on Clark Street, is the Central
Baptist Church, built in 1733. Beyond is the Armory of
the Newport Artillery, an old company, organized in
1741, and the body guard of the Governor.

The Vernon House stands on the corner of Mary and Clark Streets, and is a place of considerable interest. After the evacuation by the British, in 1779, it was the headquarters of Rochambeau, commander of the French forces. Here a grand ball and reception was given in honor of Washington.

Lafayette once occupied the house on the northwest corner of Spring and Prospect Hill Streets.

But we have wandered. Let us return to the Parade. At the head, facing the Mall, is the State House. The Assembly meets here the last Tuesday of May, each year, organizes, installs the state officers and adjourns to Providence.

Election day is a great day in the history of Newport. The whole State gathers, and the high sheriff with great pomp announces : "Hear ye! take notice that His Excellency, Governor ————, of ———— is elected Governor, Commander-in-Chief, and Captain-General of Rhode Island for the year ensuing. God save the State of Rhode Island and Providence Plantations."

This year for the first time in a space of fifty-three years, the words, "of Newport," have been inserted in the sheriff's proclamation.

The inauguration of Charles C. Van Zandt as Governor of Rhode Island was made the occasion of one of the finest celebrations held in Newport for many years. The "'Lection" day of '77 will long be remembered.

The State House, built in 1742, is after the style of the colonial architecture of the middle of the eighteenth century, and evinces considerable taste in its design. From its steps, July 20th, 1776, Major John Hardy read the Declaration of Independence, and again fifty years later the same document was read by the same individual from the same place. The building is chiefly of interest from its association with Revolutionary events. In the Senate chamber hangs the famous portrait of Washington painted by Stuart and presented by him to the town. The fine avenue leading to the left from the State House is Broadway, the old Boston Post Road.

Much of the wealth and enterprise of old Newport was due to the Jews, who in 1774 formed a large and honorable portion of the community. The Hon. William P. Sheffield, in his history of Newport, says of them:

"There were then (1774) three hundred families of Jews in Newport, represented by men of great learning, intelligence and enterprise, but they are all gone ; the dwelling houses which they erected, their synagogue and their grave-yard are the only memorials left to us of their existence. Let no vandal hand of desecration ever be laid upon that synagogue or that grave-yard, but let them remain, and keep them preserved forever as venerated memorials of a frugal and useful people, who in their day and generation contributed to the prosperity and renown of Newport."

On Touro Street, just above Spring Street, is situated the Jewish Synagogue. This synagogue, for many years the only place of Hebrew worship in America, was dedicated with great pomp and ceremony in 1763. They computed the passage of time from creation, and over the gateway is the inscription : "Erected 5,603, from a bequest made by Abraham Touro." The synagogue is not used and is kept in its present excellent condition by means of the interest on twenty thousand dollars left for that purpose by Judah Touro.

At the head of Touro Street the granite walls and handsome portal, with inverted flambeaux of the Jewish Cemetery will attract the visitor's attention. The deed to this ancient burial place is dated 1677. A liberal bequest by Judah Touro keeps it in perfect condition, and in summer it more nearly resembles a flower garden than a burial place.

> "How strange it seems! These Hebrews in their graves,
>   Close by the street of this fair sea-port town
> Silent beside the never-silent waves,
>   At rest in all this moving up and down!"

From the Cemetery following Bellevue Avenue, and passing Redwood Library, to which we will return in our next chapter, we find ourselves in Touro Park. Here is the Old Stone Mill, about which so much has been written. So many pamphlets and discussions have been showered around this old relic that all is

> "Confusion worse confounded,"

and the war of words grows fiercer ; yet the silent tower stands as it has stood and will continue to stand for ages, firm on its solid foundations, and dumb.

The structure is of unhewn stone, laid in mortar made of the gravel of the soil around, and oyster shell lime. It is of a circular form, resting upon eight round columns. It is twenty-three feet in diameter and twenty-five in height, and it is said was formerly covered with stucco. The wall above the arches is about a foot and a half thick, and is perforated with three loop-holes. On the east side is what appears to have been a fire-place, which is complete with the exception of the hearth. There was formerly a floor just above the arches, and the places where the timbers rested are distinctly visible.

The theories concerning its origin are as various as are the persons who have written of it. Certain it is that it has been used as a mill, for Governor Arnold in his will, dated December 24th, 1677, bequeaths the "Stone Mill" to his daughter.

The cement used in its structure, described by one writer as having "all the firmness of Roman mortar," it is stated has been proved by analysis to be identical with that used in all the more ancient buildings of Newport.

Professor Rafn, a high Danish authority, claims very authoratively in a work published in 1838 that the Tower is of Danish origin, and says : " That the building was erected at a period decidedly not later than the twelfth century."

It has been generally acknowledged that the Danes visited our shores long before Columbus.

Longfellow, in his " Skeleton in Armor," thus speaks of the Old Mill :

> " Three weeks we westward bore,
> And when the storm was o'er,
> Cloud-like we saw the shore
>   Stretching to leeward;
> There for my lady's bower
> Built I the lofty tower,
> Which, to this very hour,
>   Stands looking seaward."

This beautiful ballad has so pleasantly associated it with the mythology of the North that no amount of philosophical, or scientific, or historical skepticism can ever wrench it from this popular association,

It is one of the few, if not the only object in America, the date of whose origin has been lost, and the imagination loves to connect it with the wild wanderings and daring prowess of the old Viking Kings.

The hand of later generations may have destroyed its original integrity, but the more modern fire-place, embrasures, windows and apertures do not necessarily negative the assumption of great antiquity.

Near the Tower facing the avenue is the Perry Monument, erected by August Belmont at a cost of nearly thirty thousand dollars.

Next to Thames street, there is probably no thoroughfare more ancient than Long Wharf.

It runs from the foot of the Parade directly west. About one-half its length from Thames Street, where is now the new city wharf is Gravelly Point, where in 1793 twenty-six pirates were hung.

THE POINT is that portion of Newport lying north of Long Wharf and west of Thames Street. Washington is the principal street on the Point, and runs parallel with the bay. It is noted for being a quiet retreat, much sought after by literary characters.

There are many fine places on this street, all of them commanding a very fine view of the harbor. The Hunter House and Fort Greene on the street are places of historical interest. The former the home of Dr. William Hunter, being the house in which the Chevalier DeTernay expired. At the northern limit of Washington Street is the North Battery, now known as Fort Greene.

This fort was built in 1776, and did good service in compelling the British ship Scarborough to beat a hasty retreat. It was fortified during the war of 1812. The wall to the sea still remains, but the fort is in ruins and dismantled.

At the north end of the harbor and connected with Rhode Island by a bridge, lies Coaster's Harbor Island. This island was given to the poor of Newport by Governor Coddington, and on it is situated the Newport Almshouse. The land is extremely valuable, but on account of the nature of the bequest is not available for other purposes than the one for which it is now used.

At the head of Thames Street is the lot on which stood the Liberty Tree, dedicated to the Sons of Liberty by one William Read, in 1766. One clause in the deed of the place reads: "And, in general, said tree is hereby set apart for such other purposes as they, the true-born Sons of Liberty, shall, from time to time, from age to age, and in all times and ages hereafter, apprehend, judge, and resolve may subserve the glorious cause of Public Liberty."

The original tree was destroyed by the British, and another planted in 1783. That likewise was cut down, the trunk of which is in the possession of Mr. George H. Norman.

A young elm was set out in the same spot, with appropriate ceremonies, by his Honor, Mayor Bedlow, on the Centennial Anniversary of our Independence.

Near the Liberty Tree, on Thames Street, is the large white house once occupied by Hon. William Ellery, one of the signers of the Declaration of Independence. The house, if we are rightly informed, is still occupied by his descendants.

The Channing House, erected in 1720, now occupied by the United States Engineer Corps, is on Thames Street, not far from the Gas Light building.

There are also many other buildings on Thames Street that have a history ; in fact there is scarcely one that does not have a tale worthy to be told. But detail is already growing tedious, and we will only call your attention to the oldest house in Newport, situated on Spring Street, just north of Sherman, and turn our attention to Trinity Church. This church was erected in 1726, and is one of the oldest in our country. But few changes have been made in it since that time. The same large, square pews, the hexagonal sounding-board over the pulpit, which with the clerk's pew and reading desk stand far down the aisle are still there. The chancel, save the lion and unicorn torn away by patriots, remains as in 1726. The organ, bearing date 1733, was the gift of Dean Berkeley.

The ancient cemetery connected with the church is an object of much interest. Some of the graves bear dates two hundred years ago. Here rest the remains of Chevalier DeFayelle, aid-de-camp to Lafayette, and many other men whose names are illustrious.

The church is now the fashionable one of Newport, and during the "season" at the close of service, two hundred waiting carriages may be seen at its gates. Not far from here, on the northeast corner of Spring and Pelham Streets, stands the old house once the headquarters of General Prescott. There are many other famous buildings in and around Newport, and for their description we must refer the curious reader to the many works on Newport to be found in the numerous libraries of the place.

Chapter 5.

AROUND THE ISLAND.

THE DRIVES—BELLEVUE AVENUE—FINE RESI-
DENCES—OCEAN DRIVE—LILY POND—KAY
STREET—CATHERINE STREET—WASHINGTON
STREET—GLEN—LAWTON'S VALLEY—BUTTS'
HILL—TAMMANY HILL—THE DUMPLINGS—
SAILING—FISHING—POLO.

NE of the most attractive features in Newport
life is driving. One can ride for miles along the
shore where land and sea combine to render it
one of the most magnificent drives in the country,
or turning in the other direction can wander over the
island to Lawton's Valley or the Glen, passing many
choice bits of farm and inland scenery.

Many of the chief charms of the place can only be enjoyed while riding. Neither expense nor pains are spared
by the summer residents on their turn-outs. Their
coaches are the finest that money can obtain ; their
horses the fleetest. And as they ride to be seen as well
as for the pleasure, the toilets are far from being neg-
lected. The scene during fashionable hours is brilliant,
picturesque and exciting. Bellevue Avenue is the fashionable, and therefore the popular drive. From five to

seven are *the* hours, and nothing is more thoroughly enjoyable than a drive on the avenue at that time.

The Jewish Cemetery, Redwood Library, Old Mill and Ocean House, are places of interest that will be passed on the avenue, and have each been described.

From the Ocean House south to the end of the island are many of the residences that make Newport famous. The grounds belonging to most of these places are extensive, and every one of them with their long winding approaches and dense mass of foliage and bloom, would make glad the heart of a horticulturist.

On the left, just south of LeRoy Avenue is the elegant stone chateau of Mr. George Peabody Wetmore, of New York. This is the most substantial and expensive residence in Newport. On the opposite side of the avenue and only a short distance beyond, is the villa of Loring Andrews. This villa is the largest on the avenue, and the Swiss architecture of the gateways and peculiar design of the house cannot fail to arrest the attention of the passer by.

Near here and opposite, are the summer residences of A. Belmont, Geo. Bancroft, the historian, D. Parish and A. D. Jessup. The latter known as the Barreda mansion, costing nearly half a million of dollars.

Turning the avenue we come to some of the most elegant places on the drive—conspicuous among them being the fine country seats of John Paine and Gardiner Brewer. The situation of these cottages is very fine, the grounds running back to the sea. At the end of the avenue is the residence of Mrs. George Francis Train, and the Swiss *chalet* of her father, Colonel George T. M. Davis.

In the immediate vicinity are Bailey's Beach and Spouting Cave. The handsome brown cottage overlooking the sea, just back of the cave is "The Rocks," the summer house of General R. B. Potter. On the rocks in front of General Potter's residence, after a storm, great crowds assemble to witness the grand scene at Spouting Cave. The coast here resembles that of Maine, and after a storm the scene is of the wildest nature. The waves race and break, foam and tumble over one another until reaching the mouth of the cave with a roar of the loudest thunder, great clouds of spray and foam are thrown full a hundred feet into the air.

To the east Coggeshall Ledge is white with foam ; west, Brenton's Reef Light-Ship tosses like a chip on the waves ; and away to the south, through the lifting clouds you catch sight of some ship struggling to reach the haven.

Ocean Drive is a continuation of Bellevue Avenue, and is without doubt the most picturesque and fascinating of them all.

This drive (plainly marked on our map,) although at times dusty, will always give abundant satisfaction. The drive is some six or seven miles long, and for its full enjoyment plenty of time must be allowed. It winds up and down, over and around hills and mounds, giving glimpses now of land, now of sea, in the most enchanting manner. After reaching the Neck a detour to the right is made, passing the villa of Thomas Winau, and Bateman's popular hotel.

Castle Hill is just here, and rude grave-stones mark the resting place of "unknown" sailors sent ashore by the waves. From here the drive leads past Fort Adams by the way of Harrison and Carroll Avenues to Thames Street and the city.

On Harrison Avenue the residence of Jerome Napoleon Bonaparte is passed. From the junction of Harrison and Carroll Avenues south, may be seen Lily Pond, a handsome sheet of water famous for its perch fishing.

While the avenue is *the* drive of the place, there are many other streets that are quite as inviting, and should by no means be passed by. Kay Street is one of the most frequented, it being in fact a continuation of the main avenue. It makes a slight turn at the junction of Touro Street and Bellevue Avenue, and is a broad well paved thoroughfare, lined on either side with pleasant yards and fine cottages.

At the head of the street on Mann Avenue is the stone mansion of the New York banker, Mr. A. S. Hatch.

Catherine Street is another of the shady retreats that are far more pleasant than the crowded and dusty avenue. On the corner of this street and Rhode Island Avenue is the cottage, the home of the celebrated actress, Miss Charlotte Cushman, during the last years of her life.

To the stranger there can be no more interesting study of "ancient" Newport than is afforded by a ride through her streets.

Passing down Church Street from the hill to Thames Street, we pass Trinity Church and church-yard, recalling the days when we owed allegiance to a crowned head. On the left where now the *Daily News* is printed, was the wood-yard of the British during the weary years of 1776–7 and '78.

Turning north on Thames Street, the Channing House and other historical places crowd thick upon each other, until at the head of the street the Liberty Tree with its neat iron railing is passed.

Turning down Poplar we soon reach Washington Street, one of the choicest bits of scenery in all Newport. The houses here overlook the harbor and bay, and at sunset, when the water is tinged a golden hue, and the capacity of the harbor is taxed to its utmost by the yachts and fishing craft that crowd its surface, the scene is extremely picturesque. From here one can look straight out the passage to the sea, and if perchance a yacht club should be coming in you will be served with a rare treat. There is no finer sight to be seen in Newport than the incoming of some graceful vessel, with all sails set, rounding Fort Adams, and as she gains the inner harbor furling her sails and coming to anchor.

Besides the drives that lead by "old ocean," or take you on tours of inspection through the streets of the curious town, there are others that lead off over the island and past the thriving farms that cover its surface.

Of these perhaps none are so popular as the one to the Glen. The Glen is some seven miles from the city on the east side of the island, and is best reached by following Broad Street to the two-mile corner, and turning out to the right and continuing on until the Glen road is reached, down which a short distance from the main road the entrance to it will be discovered. Five miles out is the Episcopal Church, built and endowed in a liberal manner by one of the wealthy residents.

On the way to the Glen several old-fashioned windmills

with their long, ponderous and awkward arms flapping their lazy round in the summer breeze are to be seen. The wide awake tourist will see much on the way that will well repay the journey ; and when it is reached will find it " as sweet a bit of inland scenery in its way as the country affords." The old mill, worn out with age and tumbling to pieces, and large trees fallen in various directions and decaying, give the place a decidedly "old" appearance. Just before reaching the Glen is a Tea House, which will be found a " refreshing " place.

A route not so generally known but one of much historical interest, is the one that leads to Lawton's Valley, past the Overing House and on to Butts' Hill. Some five miles out on the right hand side of the road, is situated the house in which General Prescott was captured. It is of the old style of architecture so common throughout the island. The gate and path remains nearly the same to-day as in 1776, and up the ravine through which the stream that flows by the house finds its way to the sea, came the little band of Americans and stole away the British commander. A short distance further along is the pleasant valley known as Lawton's, and noted for being the summer residence of Mrs. Julia Ward Howe. In the immediate vicinity is Butts' Hill. It was here that the American forces under Generals Greene and Sullivan made their determined stand against the British when driven from the island. They had entrenched themselves at Newport and Miantinomi Hill, but owing to the withdrawal of the French fleet upon which they had depended, they were compelled to retreat to this hill. From this they retreated in good order, leaving the island in the possession of the British.

Tammany, or Miantinomi Hill lies two miles north of
the city, and is the highest ground on the island. This
hill was the seat of the government of Wannemetonomie,
an Indian sachem, and derives its name from the chief-
tain's father. The ruins of the breastworks thrown up
by the British are still to be seen. From here a chain of
outposts stretched across the island to the east passage.
At the foot of the hill was one of the most celebrated
castles of America. It was the "Malbone," built in 1744,
at a cost of one hundred thousand dollars. It was the
literary and art centre of the period. Burned in 1767 it
was never rebuilt, and nothing remains of its former magnificence. The mansion of Mayor Bedlow now stands
on almost the same spot. The view from the summit of
Tammany Hill is very fine, Fall River to the northwest
and Block Island to the southwest being easily seen on
a clear day.

Aside from riding, fishing and sailing are the popular
pastimes.

To fishing and sailing parties the Dumplings are the
most attractive places around Newport. The Dumplings
are the rocks piled in such confusion at the south end of
Conanicut Island. On these rocks is Fort Brown, known
as the Fort-on-the-Dumplings. The fort is an oval
structure about sixty by ninety feet. The outer walls,
about five feet thick, are still in a good condition, but
the inner ones are fast crumbling away and the ditches
are filled with rubbish. Four of the galleries still remain, and the port-holes overlooking the harbor remain
open. The fishing near the fort is famous, and parties
are constantly pitching their tents near the old ruins,
to enjoy a few days of genuine pleasure.

Sailing in the harbor is very fine. The services of numberless retired sailors, capable, and full of strange stories of every land, can be obtained to pilot you over the bay.

Rose Island, lying northeast of Conanicut is the sight of another Revolutionary fort. Every island and elevation had its fortification during the struggle of 1776.

The Westchester Polo grounds are at the south end of Thames Street, and while a game is in progress are the centre of attraction. Through the exertions of this club "Polo Day" during the season of 1876 became as popular as "Fort Day." The game is an exciting one, as well to the spectators as to the participants. Three games each week are usually played, and on "Polo Day" the grounds and rocks near by which form an amphitheater overlooking the grounds, are crowded with spectators.

With fishing, sailing, driving and sight-seeing a dull moment need not be spent in Newport.

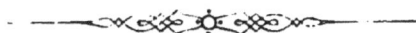

Chapter 6.

BUILDINGS AND INSTITUTIONS.

CHURCHES AND SOCIETIES—REDWOOD LIBRARY —FREE LIBRARY—SCHOOLS—MERCURY—DAILY NEWS.

For the benefit of visitors we insert a directory of the churches and principal buildings:

Protestant Episcopal.

TRINITY—Spring and Church, (corner); KAY CHAPEL—Church and High streets; REV. G. J. MAGILL.
ZION—Touro and Clarke streets; REV. E. H. KETTELL.
EMMANUEL FREE CHURCH—Spring street; REV. R. B. PEET.
ALL SAINTS' CHAPEL—Beach street; REV. DR. MERCER.
CHAPEL OF ST. JOHN THE EVANGELIST—Poplar street.

Methodist.

FIRST CHURCH—Marlboro street; REV. E. M. SMITH.
THAMES STREET CHURCH—Thames and Brewer sts.; REV. W. T. HARLOW.
TOURO CHAPEL—Bellevue avenue; REV. T. G. YEISER.

Baptist.

FIRST CHURCH—Spring street; REV. C. E. BARROWS.
SECOND CHURCH—Farewell street; REV. ————.
CENTRAL CHURCH—Clarke street; REV. N. J. WHEELER.
SHILOH—School street; REV. H. N. JETER.

Congregational.

UNITED CHURCH—Spring and Pelham streets; REV. ————.
UNION CHURCH—Division street; REV. M. VAN HORNE.

Unitarian.

Mill street; REV. J. C. KIMBALL,

Friends' Meeting House.

Marlboro street.

St. Mary's Catholic.

Spring and Levin street; REV. PHILIP GRACE.

Libraries.

REDWOOD—Bellevue avenue and Redwood street; B. H. RHOADES, Librarian.
FREE LIBRARY—178 Thames street, up-stairs; HOWARD BARKER, Librarian.
NEWPORT READING ROOM—Bellevue avenue and Church street.

Schools.

ROGERS' HIGH SCHOOL—Church street; F. W. TILTON, Principal.
CODDINGTON SCHOOL—Mill street.

Public Buildings.

POST-OFFICE—Corner Thames and Franklin Streets.
STATE HOUSE—Washington square, east side.
OPERA HOUSE—Washington square, south side.
CITY HALL—Corner Washington square and Thames street.

Masonic Societies.

WASHINGTON COMMANDERY KNIGHTS TEMPLARS. Regular Assemblies,
third Wednesday in each month, in Masonic Hall.
DEBLOIS COUNCIL ROYAL AND SELECT MASTERS—Regular Convocation,
first Tuesday in April, June, September and December, in Masonic Hall.
SAINT JOHN'S LODGE, No. 1. Regular Communication, Monday preceding full
moon, in Masonic Hall.
SAINT PAUL'S LODGE, No. 14. Regular Communication, Monday evening following full moon, in Masonic Hall.

Odd Fellows.

AQUIDNECK ENCAMPMENT. Regular Meeting, third Thursday in each month,
in Odd Fellows' Hall.
RHODE ISLAND LODGE, No. 12. Meets Monday evening, in Odd Fellows' Hall,
over Ward's bookstore.
ESTHER LODGE DAUGHTERS OF REBEKAH. Meets in Odd Fellows' Hall,
Tuesday evenings.

Knights of Pythias.

REDWOOD LODGE, No. 11. Regular Meeting every Wednesday evening, in
Pythian Hall, over Exchange Bank.

Grand Army of the Republic.

STEVENS' POST, No. 2. Meets every Wednesday evening, in Cary's Hall, 198 Thames street.

CHARLES E. LAWTON POST, No. 5. Hall over Taylor's Pharmacy. Meets every third Wednesday in each month.

Telegraph Companies.

WESTERN UNION TELEGRAPH COMPANY. Office, Cottrell's Building, Thames street. George W. Flagg, Manager.

FRANKLIN TELEGRAPH COMPANY. Office, 109 Thames Street. J. D. Proud, Manager.

Newport was born of the struggle for freedom of worship, and as a consequence we find at an early date churches of all denominations being established.

Jew and Gentile worshipped as they chose, and the Quaker and High Churchman claimed for themselves and granted to each other perfect freedom in the mode of worship.

The oldest church in the place, and probably the oldest in the State is the First Baptist, situated on Spring Street, just back of the State House. An old historian tells us that a "Baptist Church was founded in Newport in 1644, by Mr. John Clark, a leading character among the early settlers." Many claim the society to have been organized as early as 1638.

On the corner of Meeting and Farewell Streets stands the Second Baptist Church, the outcome of a quarrel in the First Church in the year 1656.

The Central Baptist Church occupy what was formerly the Second Congregational Church, on Clark Street. The society was organized in 1847. Their meeting-house is closely associated with the name of the Rev. Dr. Stiles, who was pastor of the Second Congregational Church, and who afterwards became President of Yale.

In his diary for 1666 we find this curious bit in regard to Dr. Franklin and electricity: "Dr. Franklin's Electrical Points were erected atop the spire of my steeple. From the iron spindle there descended two lines of iron rod or wire adown the N. E. and S. E. corners of the steeple to the ground."

The points were of large brass wire, extending about a foot above the vane. They are the first and only electrical rods erected in the Colony of Rhode Island, upon any Meeting House, or any public buildings, and I think there is but one private house in the Colony guarded with them. In Boston, Cambridge, and a few other places in New England, points have lately been erected upon a few Meeting Houses and the Colleges."

The Shiloh Baptist is a fourth society of this sect, and is situated on the corner of Mary and School Streets.

Of Trinity Church, erected in 1702, we have alreayd spoken, but there is so much of interest connected with this edifice that we add a few lines here. In 1724 the original structure was presented to Norwich, and the present one built at a cost of ten thousand dollars. The church received considerable aid from the old country. The first pastor, Rev. James Honyman, was sent over by the "Society for Propagating the Gospel in Foreign Parts." The edifice is "handsomely finished on the outside, and the inside pewed well, but not beautiful." The bell in the tower was presented by Queen Anne, and the organ was presented by Dean Berkeley. Zion Church, organized in 1833, is a branch from Trinity. Their house of worship is corner Touro and Clark Streets, and the society is in a prosperous condition. A still later branch is the Emmanuel Free Church. All the pews in this house are free, the expenses being defrayed by contribution or subscription. The society was organized in 1851.

The date of the Society of Friends in Newport goes back almost to that of the First Baptist Church. In 1676 we read of their monthly meetings. Their meeting-house on Marlboro Street was built in 1699. Many of the most influential members of the colonial council were of the society of the Quakers, and their broad brims are often met and always respected in the streets of Newport to-day. The First Congregational Church was founded in 1720.

In 1728 the Second Congregational Church was organized, with Dr. Ezra Styles as pastor. In 1833 the two bodies united and formed the present Congregational society, whose house of worship is situated corner of Spring and Pelham Streets.

The Union Congregational Church have a very pleasant place of meeting on Division Street. The Society was organized in 1824, and was the first church for colored people in Newport. The Methodist Episcopal Church, located on Marlboro Street, was erected in 1806. The first pastor was settled in 1805. In 1849 the colored population organized for themselves, and later in 1855, the Thames Street Methodist Church was opened.

The Unitarian Society was organized under Dr. Channing, in 1833. In 1835 they purchased the edifice on Mill Street, then occupied by the First Congregational Church. The society was for many years under the pastorate of the Rev. Charles T. Brooks, the poet preacher. It is now under the charge of Rev. J. C. Kimball.

St. Mary's (Catholic) Church, organized in 1850, stands at the corner of Spring and Levin Streets. In connection with the church is Father Grace's school, having an attendance of some five hundred pupils.

REDWOOD LIBRARY. No building in Newport has more of interest within its walls than this structure. It received its first impetus from a literary society organized in 1735. This society was brought into being through the efforts of Dean Berkeley, and had for its object the discussion—"indecency and order of some useful question in divinity, morality, philosophy, history, etc." Of Bishop Berkeley, an old writer says, in connection with this society : " He proposed many of its themes ; he took a reserved and dignified share in its conferences ; he derived an exquisite happiness, much less from his own consciousness of superiority, than from an opportunity for discerning and developing nascent literary talent, and confirming and invigorating every germ of rational faith and Christian charity. Under a leader and lecturer like Berkeley, he, the presiding genius, it is hardly to be doubted that this, the oral, is the best mode of instruction."

In 1747 Abraham Redwood gave five hundred pounds sterling for the purchase of books, Henry Collins donated the land, and shortly after the town raised five thousand pounds sterling for the library building. Of this building : " The library building, which is a beautiful specimen of the Doric order, was commenced in 1748 and completed in 1750. The plan was furnished by Joseph Harrison, Esq., assistant architect of Blenheim House, England. He also superintended the erection of the edifice with the

3

Committee of the Company, consisting of Samuel Wickham, Henry Collins, and John Tillinghast. The master-builders were Wing Spooner, Samuel Green, Thomas Melville and Israel Chapman. The principal front is ornamented with a portico of four Doric columns, seventeen feet in height, and projecting nine feet from the walls of the building. The edifice consists of a main building and two small wings on each side, ranging in a line parallel with the west end of the building. The wings furnish two rooms of about twelve feet square. The principal library room, occupying the whole of the main building, is thirty-seven feet long, twenty-six feet broad, and nineteen feet in height. The whole building is supported by a substantial foundation raised several feet from the ground."

In 1838 ten thousand dollars of stock was issued, and five thousand of this sum was expended enlarging the building. In 1876 a reading-room was added. The library has received many generous gifts. The King of England contributed eighty-four volumes. Among them will be found Dooms-Day Book, and many others, valuable because now out of print. The Revolution left the library like everything else in and around Newport in a sad condition. And for many years the library was closed. In 1810 James Oglive, a Scotchman, becoming interested in it, aroused the people, gave a course of lectures for the benefit of the library, and its doors were once more thrown open. The library now contains nearly twenty thousand volumes, and is rich in rare and valuable books. The walls are hung with valuable paintings, most of them belonging to the collection donated by

Charles B. King, a Washington artist. A Newporter, Edward King, enriched the halls with a large number of pieces of statuary, among which is a fine copy, in marble, of the Dying Gladiator. The reading-room has become quite a feature, the tables being supplied with the best literary and newspapers of the day, and leading reviews and magazines. The rooms are open to the inspection of visitors, and by paying the proper fees the use of the library can be obtained.

The Free Library, supported by the interest of a fund donated by Christopher Townsend, is on Thames Street, just above Pelham, and is free to all residents of Newport and visitors. The Library consists of over seventeen thousand volumes, and the reading-room contains the best newspapers and periodicals.

The first free school in America was organized at Newport, in 1641, and from that day to the present time the schools in the place have been of a high order. The two finest school buildings in town are the Rogers' High School, on Church Street, and the Coddington School, on Mill Street. The former is one of which all Newporters are proud. William Sanford Rogers left one hundred thousand dollars, with which fund the house was built and the school is maintained. F. W. Tilton is master of this school, and Thomas Clarke is principal of the public schools.

The story of the progress of the art of printing occupies a conspicuous place in the history of our country, and the press in Newport is a very interesting chapter of that story. The first press used in Newport was of that style known as the "Ramage Patent," and was brought over from England by James Franklin, in 1716. It was first used in Boston, the *Boston News Letter* being printed on it, Benjamin Franklin being employed as type-setter.

Afterwards James Franklin was ordered out of the Massachusetts Colony for printing libellous matter in the *New England Courant*, and settled in Newport. Here, in 1732, he commenced the issue of the *Rhode Island Gazette*, and continued its publication up to the time of his death, which occurred in 1734. The printing-office was continued by Ann Franklin, his widow, many of the colonial laws bearing her imprint.

James' son James, nephew of Benjamin, issued the first copy of the *Mercury* the 12th of June, 1758. From that time until about 1800, the press brought over by James Franklin in 1716 was used in printing the *Mercury*. In December, 1776, the press was buried in a garden on Broad Street to hide it from the British. It was discovered by them, and for three years the *Rhode Island Gazette* was printed by one John Howe, printer to His Majesty. In 1780 Henry Barber purchased the press and again issued the *Mercury*. The *Mercury* is thus the oldest paper in America. It is at present published by John P. Sanborn, and is a very readable paper, having a wide circulation in the southern part of the State. The original press—a curious piece of mechanism, and of interest from being the press on which Benjamin Franklin first worked—is the property of John B. Murray, of New York, and is in the possession of the Massachusetts Mechanics' Association, of Boston.

The *Newport Daily News*, first issued in 1846, is a wide-awake and spicy daily paper, containing all the local news, and having an extensive circulation among both the permanent and summer residents. Messrs. Davis & Pitman are the publishers, who also publish the *Newport Journal*, a weekly of considerable influence.

Chapter 7.

ACCOMMODATIONS AND CONNECTIONS.

OCEAN HOUSE — AQUIDNECK HOUSE — PERRY
HOUSE — UNITED STATES HOTEL — RESTAU-
RANTS—OLD COLONY STEAMBOAT COMPANY—
OLD COLONY RAILROAD — WICKFORD LINE—
AMERICAN STEAMBOAT COMPANY—BURTON'S
" BUS " LINE.

NEWPORT is deficient in hotel accommodations.
The few that are in the place compare favorably
with those of any other watering place; but they
are few in number, and not one of them com-
mands a sea view. The Ocean House, the largest, and
having accommodations for five hundred guests, is situated on the avenue, but save its name nothing around
it suggests the ocean.

Of those now open, this is the largest and most fashionable. It is thrown open about June 15th, of each
year, and remains so some three months. This house
was built at a considerable expense, and every possible
effort has been put forward to make it attractive and
comfortable. Concerts are given each evening under
the leadership of Professor Hall, Boston; and Saturday
evening a hop is given. The hotel is under the efficient
management of Mr. Weaver.

The Aquidneck House, on Pelham Street, is a smaller, but very popular hotel. For those who wish quiet and comfort; the rest and ease supposed to be obtained at a watering place, the Aquidneck will be found the most attractive. The hotel, the property of Mr. Philip Rider, opens early in May, and closes late in the season.

The Ocean House and Aquidneck House are the only two exclusively summer hotels in Newport, excepting, perhaps, the Cliff Hotel. The latter is situated on the cliffs near the beach, and more nearly approaches to the idea of a seaside hotel than the others. Unfortunately it is limited in capacity and is early filled with guests for the season. Connected with this hotel are the Cliff cottages. These are very popular and early filled with summer guests. The exclusiveness of a cottage is combined with the comfort and ease of hotel life. The occupant of the cottage has but to give the order, and at the appointed hour his meals are found ready on the table. Everything is prepared at the hotel, relieving the cottager of all care.

The Perry House, on Washington Square, and United States Hotel, corner Thames and Pelham Streets, are both open the entire year, and although "business" hotels, they have a large summer patronage. The Perry House, on Washington Square, has been lately refitted, and having changed hands is fast gaining upon the public confidence. The rates at these hotels will be found as moderate as those of like places. At the Ocean House and Aquidneck, regular rates are five dollars per day. The charges at United States or Perry House are more moderate.

There are numerous boarding houses scattered through the city, many of them large and finely situated. Board in these can be obtained at rates ranging from ten dollars to fifteen dollars per week.

The restaurants are numerous, and can be found to suit all tastes and to accommodate any pocket-book. Munchinger's, on Bellevue Avenue, is first class in every respect, and has a wide patronage. The restaurants having the largest patronage are to be found on Thames Street. Of these, the Ambrose Dining Rooms, just north of the Parade, is probably the best. The temperance people have lately opened a Holly Tree Coffee House on the corner of Commercial Wharf and Thames Street. This institution is under the control of the Reform Club, and although the visitor may not need to be thrown under the influence of the club, the best cup of coffee to be obtained in Newport will be found at these rooms.

Newport is most fortunate in having so many and pleasant means of communication with the surrounding large cities. Leading, of course, is the Old Colony Railroad and Steamboat Company. The fleet of the Old Colony Steamboat Company consists of the four elegant steamers, Bristol, Providence, Old Colony, and Newport. The Bristol and Providence run during the summer months, and are the ones best known to travelers. A force of nearly three hundred men have been busy the entire winter refitting and decorating these boats, and they are justly styled "floating palaces." They start from their pier, No. 28, North River, New York, at five o'clock in the afternoon, arriving in Newport early the next morning, making connections at Fall

River with the early train for Boston. Leaving Fall River each night upon the arrival of the steamboat train from Boston, (about half-past seven in the evening,) reaching Newport at nine in the evening, they arrive in New York in season for all early trains west and south. This line is justly one of the most popular in the country, and does much to render a visit to Newport inviting. The scenery on the shores of Long Island Sound is quiet, yet in the twilight delightful. Hall's Band, of Boston, enlivens each trip, making the journey from New York to Newport a decided attraction. Before the open ocean is reached the passengers have retired to wake in Newport, unconscious that that "peril of the sea," Point Judith, has been passed. The Old Colony Railroad runs four trains, daily, each way between Boston and Newport during the season. For 1877 a special express is announced, making but two stops between the two places, and traveling the distance in one hour and forty-five minutes.

The Wickford route to New York is a convenient one, and by many preferred to the Old Colony. The Eolus, of this line, leaves Commercial Wharf at 5.30 P. M., and makes close connection at Wickford Junction with the steamboat train on the Stonington Line.

The Eolus makes four trips daily, making good connections both for New York and Providence over the Providence and Stonington Railroad. Connection is also made by this line at Kingston for Narragansett Pier.

Frequent communication is had with Providence by the American Steamboat Company. This Company make daily numerous trips to Providence and return, touching at all the more important resorts on the bay.

The fare for the round trip either way is only seventy-five cents. The Company also run the excursion boat Canonicus to Block Island, making three trips weekly, viz.: Tuesday, Thursday and Saturday, commencing Thursday July 5th. Round trip tickets one dollar.

Another route to Providence, is to Fall River by the way of the Old Colony Railroad, and from there to Providence by the way of the Providence Warren and Bristol Railroad.

To persons having but a short time to spend in Newport, B. J. Burton's line of "busses" afford an excellent opportunity to see the city. They run to every point of interest, enabling the visitor to *do* the place in a short time at small expense.

Time tables will be found in all the papers and among our advertising pages.

Chapter 8.

BLOCK ISLAND.

LEAGUES north, as fly the gull and auk,
Point Judith watches with eye of hawk;
Leagues south, thy beacon flames, Montauk!

Lonely and wind-shorn, wood-forsaken,
With never a tree for Spring to waken,
For tryst of lovers or farewells taken,

Circled by waters that never freeze,
Beaten by billow and swept by breeze,
Lieth the island of Manisses,

Set at the mouth of the Sóund to hold
The coast lights up on its turret old,
Yellow with moss and sea-fog mould.

Dreary the land when gust and sleet
At its doors and windows howl and beat,
And Winter laughs at its fires of peat.

But in summer time, when pool and pond
Held in the laps of valleys fond,
Are blue as the glimpses of sea beyond:

When the hills are sweet with the brier-rose,
And hid in the warm, soft dells, unclose
Flowers the mainland rarely knows;

When boats to their morning fishing go,
And, held to the wind and slanting low,
Whitening and darkening the small sails show—

Then is that lonely island fair;
And the pale health-seeker findeth there
The wine of life in its pleasant air.

No greener valleys the sun invites,
On smoother beaches no sea-birds light,
No blue waves shatter to foam more white!

Then, circling over their narrow range,
Quaint tradition and legend strange
Live on unchallenged, and know no change.

Old wives spinning their webs of tow,
Or rocking weirdly to and fro
In and out of the peat's dull glow,

And old men mending their nets of twine,
Talk together of dream and sign,
Talk of the lost ship Palatine.— *Whittier.*

THIS island, belonging to the Narragansetts, and bear.
ing the Indian name, Manisses, was first discovered in
1524 by Varrazano, and called Claudia, in honor of the
wife of Francis I., of France. Its present name was given
it by Adriaen Block, a Dutch sailor, who discovered it in
614. Up to the close of our Revolution the island was the
witness of many desperate scenes, and the inhabitants
were often the prey of the privateers and pirates that
infested the coast. In 1664 the island was admitted to

the government of the Rhode Island Colony. The latter warning them to " admit not of any to bear rule over them but the power of this Colony." It is on the legends associated with the early history that Whittier has founded his " Palatine," from which we quote—and Dana his " Buccaneers." As early as 1644 the people of the island commenced the struggle for a breakwater and harbor. In 1867 the subject was agitated with new vigor, the scheme was pushed with all possible energy in every direction, national and state. October 22d, 1870, their efforts were rewarded with success, and the first stone of the now excellent breakwater was laid amid rejoicings of the entire island.

This pier has been run out from the shore some twelve hundred feet, at an expense of two hundred and ten thousand dollars. During the season of 1877 it is expected that improvements costing fifty thousand dollars will be made.

Those who approach the island through the spacious harbor in one of the large excursion steamers of to-day, can scarcely form an idea of the difficulties that the Block Island fishermen were compelled to contend with. But for their skill in constructing their boats, the fisheries of the place must have been insignificant. The old harbor was composed of rows of stakes between which were alternately stone fords and deep water. The shores were extremely difficult of access, and to meet this difficulty the boats known as " double enders " were constructed. This boat is alike in stern and bow. Fitted with two masts, stepped through the thwarts, there being no deck, and having on either side lee-boards. They are

considered the best sea boats on the Atlantic coast. The
new harbor has done away with the necessity of these
peculiar boats, but they are still retained to a great extent. The harbor has given a fresh impetus to all business, and from the completion of the breakwater dates
the growth of Block Island as a summer resort. The
first impression of the island is not one to be remembered
with delight. The writer's first visit was made on a hot
August day of one of the hottest summers known for
years.

Even Newport was distressing, and as we waited for
the steamer that was to carry us out to the island, vis-
ions of a green island set in the midst of the sea came
before us. We imagined a land free from dust and heat
and all the ails of a torrid summer. The sea was quiet,
even the dreaded "ground-swell" failed, and the trip
over was pleasant—and above all—cool..

When we reached the island and commenced to climb
the bluff through sand and under a scorching sun, we
wished ourselves under way for Providence.

When we reached the top of the bluff we looked in
vain for a sheltering tree, and were greeted by a stunted,
scant and browned vegetation. We were soon, however,
seated on the broad piazza of the Ocean View Hotel,
and as we enjoyed the cool ocean breeze and watched
the passing sail, we realized one of the charms of the
place. To those desiring rest, Block Island offers as
many attractions as can be found at any of our summer
resorts. There is an entire freedom from all restraint,
elaborate toilets are the exception not the rule, and genuine rest and pleasure, so much sought after and so sel-

dom found are obtained. There are some eight or ten hotels on the island, all of them neat and comfortable, and moderate in price.

They range from the smaller ones—more appropriately denominated boarding houses—accommodating from fifteen to twenty, to the large and commodious Ocean View Hotel, lighted with gas, provided throughout with hot and cold water, and affording every modern convenience. There is enough of interest around the island to engage the attention of the most restless. The beach, two miles long, will first attract attention. It lies northwest of the steamboat landing one-quarter of a mile, and is reached from the various hotels by hacks that run at all seasonable hours. Each hotel has its private bathing-houses to which their guests have access.

The waters around the island abound in all kinds of fish known to northern waters. Cod, blue-fish, haddock, halibut, bass and bonita abound, and furnish rare sport for the summer. No true lover of the rod will visit the island without obtaining a trophy from the briny deep.

The great Salt Pond, almost dividing the island, abounds with perch and black bass. The sport is not so exciting as trolling for blue fish, but it is more lively—from fifty to one hundred frequently being caught in one hour.

Boats and every convenience for a day's fishing or sailing, either on the Atlantic or Great Pond, can be readily obtained.

The Life Saving Stations, of which there are two, will be visited by every curious caller at the island. These stations along the coast have done and are doing a noble work, and nowhere are they of greater value than here. Two hundred craft pass daily, including every sort, from the giant ocean steamer to the smallest fishing smack. From 1854 to 1868 forty-eight vessels were stranded on the coast of Block Island, with the accompanying heavy loss of life. The two stations are situated, the one near the landing, the other at the Southwest Point. The buildings are eighten by forty-two feet, and fourteen feet high. These stations are provided with provisions and bedding, and a crew of six men. The life saving apparatus consists of one surf-boat, twenty-five feet long, with crooked ends, flat, sharp bottom, shallow keel, and large air chambers; one smaller boat; a mortar carrying a line five hundred yards; lines, hawsers, etc.

From December to April the crew patrol the beach at night and during storms, and, although disbanded during summer, are subject to the call of the captains.

These stations are in the Third District United States Life Saving Station. Hon. N. Ball, Superintendent of District. Captain William P. Card is keeper of Station No. 2, at the landing, and Captain Samuel Allen, of No. 3.

There are two light-houses on the island, the one on the northern extremity being of little interest; but to one who wishes to see the island in its every mood the trip to the north end is indispensable. On the way the Clay Head Bluffs will be reached, standing far above the sea, and giving a fine panoramic view of the Summer Island Home.

The light-house on Mohegan Bluff, the southeastern point of the island, belongs to the highest class, its blaze being visible thirty miles at sea. It was built in 1872 at an expense of seventy-five thousand dollars, and has connected with it a steam syren, whose gentle voice may be heard during fogs, or Mondays, when it sings for practice. This light is worth inspection, and the obliging keeper will show and explain its mysteries to the visitor. The cliffs, on which the light-house is situated, come squarely up to the sea, are from two hundred to three hundred feet high, and extend some three miles.

The cliffs, or more properly bluffs, for they are of sand, give the island, as it is approached from the south or east, a bold and rugged appearance. The topography is peculiar; the surface is very uneven, resembling in contour the sea before a northeast gale. Scattered over the island are numerous small lakes, and near the centre the great Salt Pond. The pond covers over one thousand acres of land, and in former years has been famous as an oyster bed.

Beacon Hill, near the centre, is the highest point on the island, and is reached on the only road running across the island. Those desiring to visit the places we have mentioned can obtain carriages at any of the hotels, and although the drives and teams are not celebrated for beauty and speed, yet the farms, soil, vegetation and distant views of opposite shores and passing sail will compensate for many drawbacks. The roads around the island, however, are rapidly being improved. There is now an excellent drive along the beach, and riding is gaining favor with each season. The visitors have become so numerous that the need of better communication has been seriously felt, and September 1st, of the present

season, a daily steamer from Newport is to be put on the
route.

The arrangements for the summer are as follows:

On and after July 5, the steamer Canonicus will leave
Providence on Tuesdays, Thursdays and Saturdays at 9
A. M.; arrive at the island at 1 P. M., and return at 2.45
P. M., touching at Newport each way. The Norwich and
New London Steamboat Company will run a steamboat,
leaving Norwich on Mondays, Wednesdays and Fridays
at 8.30 A. M.; leaving New London on arrival of train
from Hartford, Springfield, Williamantic and Norwich;
and will stop at the island three hours. This boat will
touch each way at Stonington. Both boats carry the
United States mail. After September 1st a steamer
carrying the mail and passengers will run regularly to
Newport during the entire year. To those who may
desire a more extended history than we have been able to
give, the history of the island by the Rev. S. T. Liver-
more, to be issued this month, (June), is recommended.

Chapter 9.

NARRAGANSETT PIER.

EXCEPTING Newport, there is no place so widely and favorably known as "The Pier." Standing on the southeastern extremity of Rhode Island, the climate and situation are hardly surpassed on the Atlantic coast. It claims all the advantages of Newport in respect to climate, without the disadvantage of fogs. The distance from Newport by water is only nine miles, and from Block Island fifteen miles. Since the completion of the railroad from Kingston to the Pier, the connections with all parts of the country are most excellent. The place has become famous as the "City of Hotels," no less than eighteen or twenty well-regulated ones inviting the attention of the visitor. The first hotel, or rather boarding-house, was opened by one John Armstrong, in 1832. Since then the increase has been gradual but constant, until, within the last eight years, the place has been rapidly growing in popular favor, and the large number of hotels find ample business. For years before Narragansett Pier attracted attention as a watering place, it was known and resorted to as one of the finest bathing places on our coast. The beach is not surpassed by that of any other watering place. It is three miles long, and one of the hardest, safest, and smoothest known to pleasure seekers. It is by far the finest on Narragansett Bay, and probably the one most used. The summer population of Newport, as mentioned in a former chapter, is exclusive and aristocratic, and even the bathing at that place partakes of the same nature. The contrary prevails at the pier, and on pleasant days the entire hotel population, one thousand strong, turn out to enjoy the bathing. It is at this hour that Narragansett Pier, with three miles of beach, rivals Saratoga and Long Branch. The attractions of the place, aside from bathing, are many ; of these fishing, sailing, driving and hunting constitute the chief. The deep sea fishing is famous, and if a day full to the over-flowing with fun is desired, there is no better way of obtaining it than to join a fishing party under the guid-ance of some careful skipper. Fishing from the piers is also a favorite pastime with the ladies. Just back of the beach is the marsh, a royal place for gunning.

The points of interest around the Pier are so numerous and so widely separated, that riding is almost a neces-sity, and has become one of the chief attractions.

One of the most pleasant drives will lead us north over a very fine farming country, and past many spots worthy of attention. Leaving the town by Beach street, we enter upon the drive. Something over a mile out we pass the ruins of Watson's Pier, where formerly a con-siderable business was enjoyed. One mile further on is the Bonnet, a small gulf leading into the bay, famous to sporting men as a fine gunning territory Near here is Quaig Beach, a choice little bathing beach. Silver Lake, a beautiful body of clear, pure water, lies to the west of the city, and will be passed on the road to Wakefield. Near Wakefield is Sugar Loaf Mountain, looking more like a mound built by human agency than the work on nature. Legend associates it with the Narragansett Indians, many Indian relics having been found buried deep in its sides. Near here, at Matunoc, is the house in which Commodore Perry was born. One of the most interesting places near the Pier is Point Judith. This place is some five or six miles from town, and is one of the dreaded points on the coast. " Avoiding Point Judith," is considered a great inducement by all steamboat companies. The scenery here is very wild, hidden reefs run far out from the shore, and could tell many a tale of shipwreck. The light is one of the most powerful on the coast, and in connection with the light-house is a life saving station.

Two miles northwest is Salt Lake. The lake is studded with islands, and is one of the most frequented spots in the region around the Pier. Yachts can always be obtained, and for picnic parties it will be found a delightful place.

A long drive, but a thoroughly enjoyable one, and to the sportsman one not to be missed, is the drive to Perryville, some eight miles distant. Here is White Lake, famous for its large pickerel and white perch.

Narragansett Heights is a mile and a half to the northwest of Narragansett Pier, and is the site of most of the residences connected with the Pier. The "Heights" comprise a tract of about eight hundred acres of land, including a fine range of hills, running parallel with the beach, and commanding an extensive view both of land and sea. The hills stand one hundred and twenty-five feet above the sea level, and are magnificently situated for summer residences. Being high they escape many of the fogs, and enjoy the full benefit of every breeze. Over the land the scene is diverse and charming. Lake and hill alternate, and the quiet hamlets of Kingston, Peacedale and Wakefield, nestled among the hills, lend interest to the view. From Tower Hill, Newport, Block Island and Point Judith can be seen. The Heights are fast gaining ground in the popular estimation.

To the guest of a day Narragansett Pier may seem dusty, dull and uninteresting. Yet, if such a tourist will visit the beach and the Heights, he will find very much of interest. The guest of a week, however, becomes attached to the drives and rambles offered by this city-by-the-sea, and returns with the season.

The place is reached from Providence or New York by the Shore Line, and from Newport by the Eolus of the Wickford Route, which connects at Wickford and Kingston for the Pier. At this writing, (May 25th), it is expected that Narragansett Heights will be made a station on the Pier and Kingston Railroad.

Chapter 10.

OTHER RESORTS.

CONANICUT PARK — ROCKY POINT — SILVER SPRINGS—FIELD'S POINT—OCEAN COTTAGE— BULLOCK'S POINT—CEDAR GROVE—MARK ROCK.

NO sheet of water along the coast is so crowded with summer resorts as Narragansett Bay. From Providence to Block Island, every elevation, neck and inlet has its hotel and high-sounding name. Every bit of the bay and inch of the soil on either side, has its tale of adventure and romance. So far as anything in the new country can be historical, it is historical. But the company that crowd for three months the boats that ply up and down the bay are after enjoyment—and clams—not history. It shall be our endeavor to guide the "fresh hand" in his search after amusement. The three most important places of the bay have already been noted, and occupy the body of our book.

CONANICUT PARK is rapidly taking its place in the front ranks among the minor resorts on the bay. This place is situated on the north end of Conanicut Island, and has earned for itself the name "New Newport." The Park embraces five hundred acres of land, laid out in parks, drives and avenues.

MAP
OF THE
State of Rhode Island,
AND
NARRAGANSETT BAY.

OCEAN

ATLANTIC OCEAN

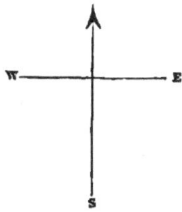

W   E

S

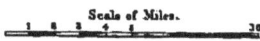

Scale of Miles.
1   2   3   4   5   20

BLOCK ISLAND
(Newport Co.)

The location is extremely pleasant, and affords a retired spot, yet having convenient means of communication with Newport. The American Steamboat Company's
boats stop each trip during both summer and winter.
Bayside avenue is a broad avenue, extending along the
shore three miles, between which and the water no
buildings are to be erected.

The views up and down the bay, and out upon "Old
Ocean" from here, are very fine. The place is cool from
constant breezes, and is freer from fogs than the larger
island.

To the general tourist the place is of little interest,
but to a family wishing a quiet and inexpensive place to
pass the summer, it offers many attractions.

Next in importance, and the one most frequented by
excursionists, is ROCKY POINT.

This place is situated some twelve or fifteen miles
south of Providence, on the west side of the bay, on
Warwick Neck. There is a very large hotel here under
the supervision of Mr. L. H. Humphries, of the City
Hotel, Providence. But the place is of chief interest
through the attractions which it offers to excursions.
During the season scarcely a day passes but that some
lodge, or school, or association crowd the grounds. It is
decidedly the most picturesque place among the many of
its kind on the bay. It is a *Rocky Point;* they are piled
in masses square to the water's edge, and, running back,
are thrown into every shape. Just back of the hotel is
a fine grove, affording ample grounds for excursion parties, and fitted up in a style to best serve their wishes.

Throughout the grounds are scattered everything that

4

can aid in making a day pleasant. Towers and caves, swings and croquet—games and amusements are furnished by the proprietors in endless variety. Connected with the place is one of the largest dining-rooms known, containing eighteen thousand square feet, and having a seating capacity for fifteen hundred people. It is quite common for ten thousand people to visit this popular place in a single day, and to prepare the clams for the immense number six great cauldrons and two mammoth ovens are constantly in use in the kitchen. Five hundred bushels of clams have been baked in one day, and persons turned away without their clams at the same time. A farm of over fifty acres is connected with the place, thus securing a fresh and constant supply of vegetables

Rocky Point will be found a very attractive place when there are no excursions; but on special occasions it is crowded beyond comfort.

During the season the American Steamboat Company's boats make almost hourly trips from both Providence and Newport.

The tourist should not fail to give this place a day of his time. As a handsome bit of scenery it is worthy of notice. As a representative of the resorts of Narragansett Bay and Rhode Island clams, it is the climax.

SILVER SPRINGS. The crowds flock to Rocky Point; but the genuine clam-eater (he who cares for his clams more than for the crowd or the trip on the bay, or rocks and trees,) goes to Silver Springs. This place is on the east side of the bay, but a few moments' ride from Providence. During the summer months the American Steamboat Company run hourly boats from Providence, and all boats from Newport make it a stopping place. it is also a station on the Providence, Warren and Bristol Railroad, and frequent trains run from their depot on India Street, Providence.

Near the Springs are favorite camping-grounds, in almost constant use. There are also pleasant surroundings, and many drive from Providence, spending the day and returning in the evening, the distance being such as to make it a very attractive trip.

The place is noted, however, as being the best place on the bay to obtain a "shore-dinner."

FIELD'S POINT is situated on the west side of the Bay, just where the Providence River flows into Narragansett Bay. This place is in charge of good hands, and, because of its nearness to Providence, has an extensive patronage. It is but a few moments' ride, the fare only ten cents from Providence and return, and during summer months merchants and clerks of Providence give it their liberal support. The table is well served, and, in an hour's time, it affords a sniff of sea air, relief from the dust and heat of a crowded city, and the luxury of a shore-dinner.

OCEAN COTTAGE is an attractive place just before reaching Silver Springs. The place is quiet. The landing is upon an island—a mass of rocks—lying just off the shore, connected with the main land by a narrow bridge. Many prefer this quiet retreat to any other on the bay.

BULLOCK'S POINT is on the eastern shore, midway between Providence and Rocky Point. The place is reached by the American Steamboat Company's boats, and is well patronized.

Other points on the bay known as " resorts," and at which shore dinners can be obtained, are : CEDAR GROVE on the east side, and MARK ROCK on the west shore.

These places are all reached by boat from Providence. There are many other hotels and resorts along the bay, accommodating from fifty to two hundred guests. But all that will be of interest to the general traveler will be found noticed in our pages. Their position can readily be traced on our excellent map of Rhode Island and Narragansett Bay, for which we are indebted to the courtesy of Messrs. J. A. & R. A. Reid, Printers, of Providence.

The following table gives the time of high tide at Newport for four months. The interval between high and low water is about six hours; between high tide and high tide twelve hours. A strong easterly wind will make a very full sea and an early tide, while a strong wind from the west will cause the opposite. High tide at Block Island is thirteen minutes, and at Narragansett Pier about thirteen minutes earlier than at Newport :

Tide Table.

	JUNE.		JULY.		AUGUST.		SEPTEMBER.
1	A. M.	7.53	A. M.	8.30	P. M.	10.15	P. M.	11.35
2	"	8.44	"	9.23	"	11.05	"	0.03
3	P. M.	10.07	"	10.16	"	11.55	"	0.58
4	"	11.03	P. M.	11.32	"	0.20	"	1.53
5	"	11.55	"		"	1.10	"	2.52
6	"	0.19	"	0.42	"	2.03	"	3.53
7	"	1.05	"	1.28	"	3.03	"	4.51
8	"	1.52	"	2.18	"	4.08	"	5.43
9	"	2.41	"	3.15	"	5.12	"	6.29
10	"	3.36	"	4.20	"	6.11	"	7.09
11	"	4.37	"	5.26	"	7.00	"	7.45
12	"	5.39	"	6.27	"	7.42	"	8.20
13	"	6.39	"	7.20	"	8.21	"	8.57
14	"	7.35	"	8.09	"	8.59	"	9.37
15	"	8.28	"	8.53	"	9.36	A. M.	9.57
16	"	9.19	"	9.37	A. M.	9.55	"	10.41
17	"	10.10	"	10.18	"	10.35	"	11.29
18	A. M.	10.35	A. M.	10.39	"	11.16	"	
19	"	11.20	"	11.19	"	11.58	"	0.44
20	"		"	11.57	"	0.20	"	1.35
21	"	0.21	"	0.16	"	1.06	"	2.31
22	"	0.58	"	0.55	"	1.55	"	3.32
23	"	1.35	"	1.35	"	2.52	"	4.35
24	"	2.15	"	2.22	"	3.55	"	5.34
25	"	3.00	"	3.17	"	5.02	"	6.30
26	"	3.51	"	4.19	"	6.04	"	7.19
27	"	4.47	"	5.24	"	6.59	"	8.07
28	"	5.46	"	6.26	"	7.47	"	8.57
29	"	6.45	"	7.22	"	8.34	"	9.51
30	"	7.39	"	8.12	"	9.22	"	10.51
31	"		"	9.10	"	10.13		

New York Yacht Club.

OFFICERS:

S. NICHOLSON KANE, Commodore.
WM. H. THOMAS, Vice-Commodore.
J. J. Alexandre, Rear-Commodore.

CHARLES A. MINTON, Secretary.
SHEPPARD HOMANS, Treasurer.
A. CAREY SMITH, Measurer.

NAME.	OWNER.	NAME.	OWNER.
Schooners.		*Sloops.*	
Alarm	A. C. Kingsland.	Active	F. W. J. Hurst.
Clio	John R. Platt.	Addie Voorhis	C. Roosevelt.
Clytie	A. B. Cook.	Alert	Henry Vail.
Clytie	Wm. L. Brooks.	Alice	T. G. Appleton.
Clochette	C. W. Galloupe.	Ariadne	Theo. A. Strange.
Columbia	Lester Wallack.	Breeze	H. P. Kingsland.
Comet	Wm. H. Langley.	Christine	F. P. Brown.
Cornelia	John R. Fell.	Coming.	S. P. Blagden.
Cruiser (Yawl	J. B. Henry.	Dudley	J. W. Russell.
Dauntless	J. Gordon Bennett.	Elaine	H. G. Russell.
Dreadnaught	Chas. J. Osborne.	Egeria	G. W. M. Sturges.
Edith	George O. Hovey.	Eugenie.	Henry Roussel.
Enchantress	J. F. Loubat.	Fanny	C. H. Mallory.
Estelle	J. D. Smith.	Fiona (Cutter	E. P. Boutcher.
Eva	E. Burd Grubb.	Gracie	John R. Waller.
Embassador	Wm. Astor.	Irene	T. D. Harrison.
Faustine	G. P. Russell.	Krimhilda	Count Batthyany.
Fire Fly (Ya'l	A. Block.	Onward	Fred'k Townsend.
Fleetwing	Geo. A. Osgood.	Pirate	Jos. Vonda.
Fleur de Lis	A. Cheney.	Recreation	Henry C. Sturgis.
Foam	T. D. Boardman	Sadie	W. E. Greenleaf.
Gypsie	H. T. Livingston.	Two Susies	Henry Harley.
Idler	S. I. Colgate.	Vindex (iron	Robert Center.
Josephine	Lloyd Phœnix.	Vision	J. J. Alexandre.
Madeleine	J. S. Dickerson	Vixen	F. C. Lawrence.
Nereid	A. P. Stokes.	Volante (Cut.	F. B. Hitchcock.
Nettie	G. H. Hepworth.	Windward	S. A. Willoughby.
Palmer	R. Stuyvesant.	*Steamers.*	
Peerless	I. R. Maxwell.		
Phanton	W. H. Osgood.	Blunderbuss.	Count Batthyany.
Rambler	W. H. Thomas.	Ermengard	G. P. Russell
Resolute	A. S. Hatch.	Fauvette.	E. Perignon.
Restless	S. N. Kane.	Gitana	Baron Rothschild.
Tarolinta.	H. A. Kent.	Ibis	John A. Brown.
Vesta	S. M. Mills.	Ideal	Theo. Havemeyer.
Viking	Mahlon Sands.	L'yof theL'ke	Sir. R. Peel, Bart.
Wanderer	James Stillman.	Lurline	Philips Phœnix.
		Minnehaha	H. I. Barbey.
		Mystic	E. S Chapin.
		Skylark.	E. S. Jaffray.
		Wyvern	William Inman.

Brooklyn Yacht Club.

OFFICERS:

J. LESTER WALLACK, Commodore.
CHAS. H. HALL, Vice-Commodore.
JOHN B. NORRIS, Rear-Commodore.
CHAS. BLOSSOM, President.
WILLIAM T. LEE, Secretary.
WILLIAM T. LEE, Treasurer.
GEORGE G. DUNNING, Asst. Sec'y.
JONN M. SAWYER, Measurer.

NAME.	OWNER.	NAME.	OWNER.
Schooners.		*Sloops.*	
Alarm	Geo. L. Kingsland.	Belle	Thomas F. Morris.
Clio	John R. Platt.	Elizabeth	Michael S. Tynan.
Dreadnaught	Chas. J. Osborne.	Fanny	C. H. Mallory.
Emily	Natha'l P. Rogers.	Florence	Rendal H. Foote.
Enchantress	I. F. Loubat.	Gracie	J. Halsey.
Estelle	J. D. Smith.	Gussie	J. D. Fowler.
Gypsie	H. T. Livingston.	Wave	John H. Dimon.
Idler	S. J. Colgate.	Kate	Geo. F. Randolph.
Leatha	Smith Ford.	Linda	John W. Stout.
Madeleine	J. S. Dickerson.	Lizzie L	J. G. Johnson, MD
Mystic	C. H. Hall.	Sadie	John B. Norris.
Rambler	W. H. Thomas.	Selene	Henry S. Wood.
Sea Witch	Frank S. Stott.	Schemer	Corn'l Lee.
Siren	C. T. Morrogh, M.D	Sophia	Chauncey M. Felt.
Tarolinta	H. A. Kent.	Susie S	E. P. Miller.
Tidal Wave	Wm. Voorhis.	Wm T Lee	Charles A. Cheever
Vesta	S. M. Mills.	Niantis	Rich'd H. Huntley
Wanderer	J. S. Stillman.	America	John J. Tredwell.
Sloops.		*Steamers.*	
Alice	H. J. Steers.	Emily	S. W. Battershall.
Ada	A. P. Bliven.	Mystic	B. S. Chapin.
Aquata	John M. Dagnal,	N. Amsterdam	C. G. Gunther.
Ariadius	Theo. A. Strange.	Tourist	C. A. Chesebrough
Arrow	R. Winans.	Virginia	F. Griswold Heron

Newport Summer Resident,

SEASON 1878.

Anderson, E J, Boston, Portsmouth, near the Glen.
Andrews, Frank W, Boston, Maple avenue.
Agassiz, Professor Alexander, Cambridge, Mass, Castle Hill.
Arnold, Hon Samuel G, Providence, East Shore, Middletown.
Appleton, Thomas G, Boston, Catharine street.
Andrews, W L, New York, Bellevue avenue.
Andrews, Constant A, New York, Bellevue avenue.
Adams, Thatcher M, New York, Marine avenue.
Anthony, Mrs. Charles L, New York, Hoppin's, Beach View avenue.
Allibone, Lieutenant Charles O, U S N, Harris's, Mill street.
Brewer, Mrs Gardner, Boston, Bellevue avenue and the Cliffs.
Brinley, E L, Philadelphia, Sunnyside place.
Bryce, J Smith, New York, Bellevue and Narragansett avenues.
Baker, Mrs Richard J, Jr, Boston, Ledge road and Ocean avenue.
Brownson, J S, New York, Tatum's, Washington street.
Bennett, J. G, New York, "Fair Lawn," Bellevue avenue.
Bates, C Francis, New York, near Coddington Point.
Bronson, Arthur, New York, near Castle Hill.
Bruen, Herman W, New York, Catherine street.
Blatchford, Judge Samuel, New York, Greenough place.
Blatchford, Mrs. R M, New York, Beachstreet and Greenough place.
Blatchford, Miss S E, New York, Catharine street.
Bancroft, John C., Boston, Livingstone's Cottage, Cliff.
Bancroft, Hon Geo Washington, D C, Bellevue ave and the Cliffs.
Barstow, J S, Boston, East Shore, Middletown.
Beach, Charles N, Hartford, Kay and Ayrault streets.
Belmont, Hon August, New York, Bellevue avenue and the Cliffs.
Bigelow, John W, New York, Washington street.
Bigelow, Joshua R. Boston, Washington street.
Bacon, Mrs D G, New York, Lawton's Valley, Portsmouth.
Bruen, Mrs Mary L, New York, Bellevue avenue.
Bryer, Benjamin, New York, Park street.
Barker, Fred, Providence, Paradise road.
Barker, William, Providence, Paradise road.
Barber, Lieut, U S A, Holmes, Bellevue avenue.
Bourne, Mrs M A, Boston, Simmon's, Broadway.
Bartlett, Professer, W H C, New York, Broadway.
Bruens, Mrs Mary, New York, Bellevue avenue.
Breese, Captain, K R, U S N, Goat Island.

Brown, George M, Boston, Maple avenue.
Bowen, Stephen, Boston, Spring and Prospect Hill street.
Baldwin, Commodore, C H. U S N, Bellevue avenue.
Brown, Mrs John A, Philadelphia, Bellevue aveand Spring street.
Becar, Alfred, New York, Titus's, Broadway.
Bronson, Mrs. Isaac, New York, Wright's, Rhode Island avenue.
Brinley, E H, Riverside, Ct, Bradford's, Catherine and Ayrault Sts.
Blight, Atherton, Philadelphia, Johnson's, Bellevue court
Brown, John A, Jr. Philadelphia, Bellevue avenue.
Brown, Alexander, Philadelphia, Bellevue avenue.
Brown, Frederick K, Philadelphia, Bellevue avenue.
Brewerton, Gen Henry, U S Engineer Corps, Case's, Catherine St.
Bradt, Mrs Julia B, Lowell, Conanicut Park.
Bryant, Gridley F J, Boston, Ocean House.
Burgess, Walter, Boston, Hazard's, Catherine street.
Bartlett, N S, Boston, Hazard's, Catherine street.
Barker, Joseph, Providence, Swamp road.
Bennett, J S, New York, No 3 Cliff Cottage.
Belmont, Perry, New York, Bellevue avenue.
Belmont, August Jr, New York, Bellevue.
Bayard, Mrs Baltimore, Kay Street House.
Barker, Commander Albert S, U S N, Hotel Aquidneck.
Cushing, Robert M, Boston, Ocean avenue and the Cliffs.
Cushing, Thomas F, Boston, Bellevue avenue and the Cliffs.
Cushing, Miss Helen F Fitchburg, Conanicut Park.
Cranston, Mr Providence, Conanicut Park.
Cahoone, Andrew, New York, Mill street.
Cleveland, Dr C, New York, Peckham's, Paradise road.
Cullum, Gen Geo W, U S Eng Corps, Seaview ave and the Cliffs.
Cushman, Edwin C, St Louis, Catherine St and Rhode Island ave.
Crownshield, General Casper, Boston, Bellevue avenue.
Crownshield, Miss H S, Boston, Bellevue avenue.
Chickering, Mrs C F, New York, Bellevue avenue.
Chickering, Mrs T E, New York, ——
Cadwallader, General George W, Philadelphia, Bellevue avenue.
Coles, W F, New York, Bellevue avenue.
Cope, Marmaduke C, Philadelphia, Washington street.
Cram, Mrs G C, New York, Paradise road.
Cooke, Professor Josiah P Jr, Cambridge, Mass, Gibbs avenue.
Coit, Rev A H, Concord, N H, Washington street.
Crow, Weyman, St Louis, Cushman's, Rhode Island avenue.
Calvert, George H, Baltimore, Kay street and Mann avenue.
Caldwell, Misses, New York, Kay and Ayrault streets.
Chanler, children of late John Chanler, New York, Cliff avenue.
Cooke, Joseph J, Providence, Bellevue avenue.
Cooper, Edward, New York, Willing's, Webster and Spring streets.
Crocker, Mrs Fitchburg, Mass, Conanicut Park.
Cook, Professor William, Cambridge, Mass, Conanicut Park.
Churchill, Chas. C., U. S. A., Ayrault street.
Courtis, Lieutenant Frank, U S N, Hotel Aquidneck.

Couden, Lieutenant Albert R, U S N, Gifford's, Clarke street.
Carpenter, Commander Charles C, U S N. Hotel Aquidneck.
Channing, Dr William F, Prov, Tuckerman ave, near the beach.
Codman, Mrs J Amory, Boston, Ocean House.
Cook, Rev Dr, New York, Ocean House.
Deacon, Miss Ida E, Boston, Bellevue avenue.
D'Hauteville, F S G, New York, Bellevue avenue.
Dickey, Judge Hugh T, Chicago, Wellington avenue.
Dickey, Charles D, New York,———
Draper, Henry, New York, Hall's Cliff House.
Draper, Mrs Simeon. New York, Hall's Cliff House.
Downing, John W, New York, Melbone House.
Davis, Mr Providence, Conanicut Park.
DeBlois, Mrs J A, Boston, Francis's, Everett place.
Davis, Col G T M, New York, Bellevue ave, near Bailey's Beach.
Dexter. S R, Warren, R I, Conanicut Park.
Drew, Mrs M G, Boston, Conanicut Park
Davies, Julian T, New York, Smith's, Paradise road.
Davis, Edmund, Providence, Anthony's, Bellevue ave and the Cliffs.
De Bert, Mme, Sweden, Moore's, Bellevue ave and the Cliffs, De-
    DeBlois's cottage.
Davis, E W. Providence, Anthony's, Bellevue avenue.
De Klenck, Baron. Germany, Lawrence's, Ochre Point.
Dana, William S, Lieutenant Commander,U S N, Hotel Aquidneck.
Edgar, William, New York. Beach street.
Eustis, Professor H S, Cambridge, Mass, Conanicut Island.
Emott, Judge James, New York, Thorp's, Wellington avenue.
Emery, Lieutenant W H, U S N, Hazard's, Catherine street.
Emery, General, U S A, Bellevue Villa, Catherine street.
Elmer, Horace, Lieutenant Commander, U S N, Dame's, Broadway.
Fearing, George R, New York, Narragansett avenue.
Fearing, Henry S, New York, Annandale road.
Fearing, W H, New York, Dale's, Buena Vista street.
Forsyth, Russell, New York, Ayrault street.
Fritsch, Hugo O, New York (Andrew's), Bellevue avenue.
Fales, George S, Providence, Paradise road.
Fales, John R, Providence, Paradise road.
Flint, Henry S, Providence, Broadway.
Foster, John, Boston, Leroy avenue.
French, Abel, New York, Bellevue avenue and the Cliffs.
Flagg, Mrs M S, New York, Robinson's, Catharine street.
Farmer, Prof M G, Cambridge, Mass, Goat Island.
Fergerson, Mrs T B, Baltimore, Whipple's, Cliff and Sea View aves.
Francis, Rev Lewis, Brooklyn, Witherbee's, Honneyman Hill.
Fellows, F W, New Haven, Gray's, Washington street.
Fairchild, Mrs F E, Morristown, N J, Ive's, Brinley street.
Fowler, Mrs Edward, Brooklyn, Vogdes's, Fort Adams.
Ford, John R, Baltimore, Harrison avenue.
Foster, Joseph, Paymaster, U S N, Paine's, Touro street.
Gibbs, Professor Walcott, Boston, Gibbs avenue.

Green, Professor, Princeton, N J, Howland's, Conanicut Island.
Gray, Mrs M E, New York, Narragansett avenue.
Gammell, Professor Wm. Prov, Narragansett ave and the Cliffs.
Green, William B, New York, Malbone avenue and Broadway.
Green, Mrs D B, Boston, Narragansett avenue.
Griswold, John N A, Boston, Bellevue avenue.
Grunhut, J, New York, Harrison avenue.
Gray, Dr John P. Utica, N Y, Wilbor's, Washington street.
Gibbes, Miss Emily O, New York, Gibbs avenue.
Gibbes, Miss Sarah B, New York, Gibbs avenue.
Green, Arnold, Providence, Potter's, near Hanging Rocks.
Gibbs, Mrs Thomas S, New York, Wilson's, Beach street.
Goddard, Frank, Providence, Ledyard's, Catherine street.
Guild, Reuben A, Providence, Conanicut Park.
Gray, Edward, Boston, Story's, Conanicut Park.
Graves, Rev H C, Fall River, Conanicut Park.
Goelet, Ogden, New York (Jones's), Bellevue avenue.
Greenough, Mrs Horatio, Boston, Kay Street House.
Gray, Rev Geo Zabriski, D D, Cambridge, Mass, Hall's, on the Cliffs.
Glidden, Geo D B, Lieutenant Commander, U S N, Perry House.
Goodrich Caspar, Lieutenant Commander, U S N, Goat Island.
Hunt, Miss Jane, New York, Ayrault street.
Hubbard, Gov, Hartford, [Probably one of the Cliff cottages.
Havemeyer, Theodore A, New York, Andrews's, Bellevue avenue.
Herrick, E J, New York, Clay and Dixon streets.
Howland, Meredith, New York, Torrance's, Bellevue avenue.
Homans, I S, New York, Gould Island, near Newport.
Hunt, Richard M, New York, Touro street and Bellevue avenue.
Hoffman, Miss S O, New York, Bellevue avenue and the Cliffs.
Hoback, Mrs Celena B, New York, Harrison avenue.
Huntington, Professor J P, Hartford, Indian avenue.
Hunnewell, Hollis H, Boston, Yznaga avenue and the Cliffs.
Hone, Robert S, New York, Russell's, Narragansett avenue.
Hart, Samuel, Philadelphia, Ocean House.
Hamilton, Schuyler, Jr, New York, Ray's, Clay street.
Hoyt, D W, Providence, Conanicut Park.
Heap, Capt D P, U S Engineer corps, Bedlow avenue.
Howard, Mrs E S, Providence, Kay and Bull streets.
Hayward, Mrs M A, Boston, Smith's, Washington street.
Harper, J W, New York, Hall's, near Hall's Cliff House.
Halleck, Henry W, New York, Sea View avenue.
Hinckley, Mrs A C, Boston, Kay Street House.
Hill, Professor W N, ———, Goat Island.
Ingersoll, Harry, Philadelphia, Reef Point and the Cliffs.
Jones, George F, New York, Harrison avenue.
Jones, Frederic, New York, Harrison avenue.
Jones, Mrs Mary M, New York, Wellington avenue.
Jones, Miss Emily, New York, Wellington avenue.
Kernochan, James P. New York, Marine avenue.
Kernochan, J Fred, New York, Narragansett avenue and the Cliffs.

Kettoltas, Mrs Eugene, New York, Webster street.
Kuower, John, New York, Bellevue avenue and the Cliffs.
Kane, Mrs DeLancey, New York, not decided.
King, Mrs Edward, New York, Bowery, Spring and Golden Hill Sts.
King, Mrs A M, Hartford, Ayrault street.
King, David, Jr, New York, Bellevue avenue.
King, Clarence, New York, Church and High streets.
Kendall, I C, New York, Washington street.
Kennedy, Miss R L, New York, Auchincloss's, Washington street.
Kortright, Mrs N G, New York, Pell's, Greenough place.
John Kendrick, Providence, Conanicut Park.
Kilton, J B, Providence, Conanicut Park.
Kimber, Henry, Philadelphia, Cops's, Washington street.
Lombard, E, U S A, Hall's Cliff House.
Ladd, John G, New York, Bath road.
Ledyard, Henry, New York, Catherine street.
Low, A A, New York, Castle Hill.
Lorillard, Pierre, New York, Lawrence avenue and the Cliffs.
LaFarge, John, New York, Sunnyside place.
LeRoy, Daniel, New York, Bellevue avenue.
LeRoy, Stuyvesant, New York, Mann avenue.
Lewis, W H, New York, Hall's, Coggeshall avenue.
Livingston, Herman T, New York, Sea View avenue and the Cliffs.
Livingston, Maturin, New York, Bellevue court.
Lyman, Charles, Boston, Webster street.
Lyman, Charles F, Boston, Leroy avenue.
Lazarus, M, New York, Bellevue avenue.
Lawrence, James G K, New York, Ochre Point.
Latrobe, Mrs Osman, Baltimore, Bateman's, Brenton's Point.
Lewis, Mrs H J, New York, Hall's Cliff House.
Lenox, James, New York, Hatch's, Kay street.
Lieber, Hamilton, New York, Terrill's, Kay street.
Low, Seth, Jr, New York, near Castle Hill.
Luther, Mrs B J, Providence, Conanicut Park.
Livingston, Mrs R L, Hyde Park, Bennett's, Catherine street.
Moore, Mrs Bloomfield N, Phila, Jessup's, Bellevue ave and the Cliffs.
Morris, Mrs Jane, Philadelphia, Washington street.
Mauran, James E, Providence, Rhode Island avenue.
Marquand, H G, New York, Rhode Island ave and Buena Vista St.
Mason, Robert M, Boston, Buena Vista treet and Bath road.
Mayer, Edward, New York, Washington street.
Miller, George M, New York, Ledge road and Bellevue avenue.
Morris, Henry G, Philadelphia, Washington street.
Morgan, Rev W F, New York, Redmond's, Kay street.
McTavish, Mrs M S, Baltimore, Weaver's, Bellevve avenue.
Mason, Perry, Providence, Conanicut Park.
Mitchell, Dr S Weir, Philadelphia, No. 4 Cliff Cottage.
McAllister, Ward, New York, Barclay's, Bellevue avenue.
Mott, Thomas, Philadelphia, Mason's, Bellevue avenue.
Moseley, Alexander, Boston, Dame's, Broadway.

McKim, Mrs Robert M Bigelow's, Washington street.
Murray, Rev Dr, Princeton, N J, Anthony's, Conanicut Island.
Mehring, Dr George, Philadelphia, Ocean House.
Maynard, Washburn, Lieutenant, U S N, Goat Island.
Maloney, Francis R, Key West, Eldred's, Church street.
Mason, Dr John, New York, Stockton's, Kay and Touro street.
McCurley, Felix, Lieutenant Commander, U S N, Hotel Aquidneck.
Mannix D Pratt, First Lieut, U S Eng Corps. Barker's, Broadway.
Nomberg. Mr, New York, [Probably one of the Cliff cottages.
Norman, Geo H, Greenough Place and Beach street.
Nugent. George, Germantown, Pa., Coggeshall avenue.
Newell, John S, Lieutenant, U S N, Goat Island.
Olyphant. Mr. New York. Howland's, Conanicut Island.
Ogden, Dr J D. New York, Red Cross avenue and Beach street.
Outrey, Max. French Minister, Russell's, Narragansett avenue.
Ogstin, Mrs H W, New York, Curtis's, Redwood street.
Perkins. C E, Boston, Bruen's, Bellevue avenue.
Pugh, Dr John H, Hartford, Indian avenue.
Peckham, Peleg, St Louis, Middletown.
Phelps, Royal, New York, Clay street
Philbrick, E S, Boston, Coddington Point.
Parish, Daniel, New York, Bellevue avenue and the Cliffs.
Prince, Colonel William E, U S A. Beach View avenue.
Phoenix, S Whitney, New York, Wellington avenue.
Penrose. Walter, Philadelphia, No 1 Cliff cottage.
Fratt, Samuel F, Boston, Bellevue avenue.
Potter, Charles T, Providence, Rhode Island avenue.
Potter, Rev H C, D D, New York, Rhode Island avenue.
Potter, General R B, New York, Ocean ave, near Spouting Rock.
Post, William, New York Hoppin's, Beach View avenue.
Peterson, C J, Philadelphia, Bath road.
Parkman, George F, Boston, Bellevue avenue.
Paine, John, New York, Bellevue avenue and the Cliffs.
Pierson, J F, New York, Bellevue avenue.
Pendleton, George H, Cincinnati, Ochre Point and the Cliffs
Pennington, Mrs Emily L, New York, Clay and Dixon streets.
Paull, W W, Philadelphia, Second and Cherry streets.
Perry, Mrs. C. G. Philadelphia, Greenough place.
Phinney, Theodore W, Chicago, Carroll avenue.
Pearsall, Thomas M, New York, Chanler's, Bath road.
Pomeroy, E C, Providence, Conanicut Park.
Parsons, Mr, Washington, No. 6 Cliff Cottage.
Porter, Dr C B, Boston, Conanicut Park.
Peckham, Dr, New York, Ocean House.
Packard, Professor, Princeton, Howland's, Conanicut Island.
Picot, Miss, Philadelphia, Kay Street House.
Post, John, New York, Havemeyer's, Bellevue avenue.
Pendleton, C H, Lieut Com, U S N, Muenchinger's, Bellevue ave.
Pendleton, Edwin C, Lieutenant, U S N, Dame's, Broadway.
Reed, G W, Boston, Bellevue avenue.

Robb, Mrs Martha, Baltimore, Bull street.
Russell, Charles H, Jr, New York, Narragansett avenue.
Rives, William O, Boston, Red Cross avenue.
Russell, Mrs W H, New York, Narragansett avenue.
Russell, Charles H. New York, Narragansett avenue.
Rives, William C. Jr, Boston, Red Cross avenue.
Robinson, Clarence, New York, Brightman's, Central court.
Rice, E, Boston, Pelham street.
Rhinelander, F W. New York, Redwood street.
Rogers, Professor William B, Cambridge, Mass, Gibbs avenue.
Rogers, H. B. Boston De Blois's, Catherine street.
Rogers, Prof Fairman, Philadelphia, Ochre Point and the Cliffs.
Ray, Robert. New York, Clay street.
Redmond, William, New York, Peckham's, Indian avenue.
Rogers, Maxon, Boston, east shore, Middletown.
Rogers, John, Boston, Eustis's. Gibbs avenue.
Ramsay, Captain F M, U S N, Rodman's, Touro street.
Remey, George C, Commander, U S N, Hotel Aquidneck.
Rockwell, Charles H, Lieut Commander, U S N, Hotel Aquidneck. .
Spink, Ray, Providence, Rhode Island avenue.
Stevens, Frederic W, New York, Bellevue avenue.
Sheldon, Frederic, New York, Narragansett avenue.
Sherman, W Watts, New York, Shepherd avenue
Schermerhorn, E H, New York, Narragansett avenue and Clay St.
Sandford, M H, New York, Washington street.
Sands, Mahlon, New York, Ledge road and Ocean avenue.
Sands, Mrs A B, New York, Ledge road and Ocean avenue.
Sands, Mrs A L, Catherine street and Greenough place.
Schuyler, Philip, New York, Bellevue avenue.
Scholes, H B. Brooklyn, Bellevue avenue.
Stout, F A, New York, Bellevue avenue and the Cliffs.
Shaw, Quincy A, Boston, Castle Hill.
Stout, Mrs A G, New York, Bellevue avenue and the Cliffs.
Story, Franklin H, Boston, Potter's, Catherine street.
Sigourney, Mrs M B, Boston, Bellevue avenue.
Sigourney, Henry, Jr, Boston, Bellevue avenue.
Smith, F S, Providence, Bellevue court.
Stead, Frank D, Providence, Conanicut Park.
Swann, ex-Governor Thomas, Baltimore, Cliff and Sea View ave.
Swift, W H, New York, Parkinson's, Bellevue avenue.
Sampson, E C, New York, Smith's, Washington street.
Shields, Prof Charles W, Princeton, N J, Waring's, Catherine St.
Seely, Commander H B, U S N, Hammett's, Conanicut Island.
Schermerhorn, Rev M K, Poughkeepsie, N Y, Slocum's, Kay street.
Sage, E, Paine's, John street.
Shaw, George R, New York, Mason's, Bellevue avenue.
Sheffield, Theodore, New York, Barker's, Paradise road.
Simpson, Commodore Edward, U S N, Ive's, Brinley street.
Smith, Henry J, Providence, Bellevue court.
Slowdem, General R, Washington, Hall's Cliff House.

Schofield, Mrs General, U S A, Ennis's, Pelham street.
Stearns, Dr, Baltimore, Guild's, Mill street.
Sargent, Mrs N L, Boston, Tew's, Brinley street.
Selfridge, Mrs Captain T O. U S N, Riggs', Catherine street.
Shea, Judge George, New York, Hodges', Catherine street.
Stanton Oscar F, Commander, U S N, Hotel Aquidneck.
Swayne, Judge, Washington, No 6 Cliff cottage.
Stevens, T H, Lieutenant, U S N, Hotel Aquidneck.
Stevens, Mrs Paran, New York, Bellevue avenue and Jones court.
Tailer, Mrs Henry A, New York, Bellevue avenue.
Tiffany, George, Baltimore, Narragansett avenue and Clay street.
Tudor, Henry, Boston, Carry's, Channing avenue.
Tucker, W W, Boston, Bellevue av nue and the Cliffs.
Travers, William R, New York Narragansett and Lawrence ave.
Tatum, Samuel C, Cincinnati, Washington street.
Taylor, Rear Admiral, U S N, Gilpin's, Thames street.
Torrance, Daniel, New York, Bellevue avenue.
Ticknor, Miss Anna E, Boston, Hall's, Annandale road.
Tyler, George F, Philadelphia, Bellevue court.
Tompkins, Hamilton B, NewYork, Redwood street.
Thorne, Jonathan, Jr, New York, Chanler's, Bath road.
Thayer, Nathaniel, Jr, Boston, Wales', Yznaga ave and the Cliffs.
Tayler, Dr Isaac E, New York, Gray's, Bellevue avenue.
Taber, John R, New York, Peckham's, Paradise road.
Tennant, D B, Petersburg, Va, Hall's on the Cliffs.
Ticknor, Mrs George, Boston, Hall's, Annandale road.
Tabor, Charles F. Providence, Conanicut Park.
Thurston, G R, Smith's, Washington street.
Thackara, Alex M, Lieut, U S N, Muenchinger's, Bellevue avenue.
Upham, Mrs S F. Boston, Dunnell's, Rough Point.
Vanderbilt, W K, New York, Train's, Bellevue avenue.
Voorhis, Mrs Jacob, New York, Hogan's, Howard avenue.
Von Rosen, Baron, Sweden, Moore's Bellevue ave and the Cliffs.
Watson, Dr W Argyle, New York, John and Spring streets.
Whiting, Mrs Sarah S., New York, Bellevue avenue and Weber St.
Whiting, Augustus L, New York, Bellevue avenue.
Winn, Mrs A E Philadelphia, Cherry street.
Wilson, Professor James, New York, Cottage and Redwood Sts.
Wolfe, Miss C L, New York, George, Mill and Pelham streets.
Willing, Edward S, Philadelphia, Webster and Spring streets.
Willing, Richard L, Philadelphia, Red Cross avenue.
Willett, Mrs E M, New York, Catherine street.
Woodworth, Mrs. A P, New York, Retirement road and Cliff ave.
Winthrop, Buchanan, New York, Knight's, Bellevue avenue.
Willard, E W, Chicago, Beach View avenue.
Wheeler, C J, Philadelphia, Second street.
Whittaker, William, Providence, Paradise road.
Wilbour, Job, Providence, Green End, Middletown.
Woods, Marshal, Providence, Bellevue avenue.
Williams, Captain J, Providence, Conanicut Park.

Witherbee, Walter, New York, Honneyman Hill.
Whipple, John, New York, Cliff and Sea View avenue.
Witherbee, Silas H, New York, Honneyman Hill.
Whitney, Miss, New York, Kernochan's, Narragansett avenue.
Whitney, Mrs, New York, Kernochan's, Narragansett avenue.
Williams, Capt J, Providence, Conanicut Park.
Woodrow, Rev S G, Providence, Conanicut Park.
Wyett, Mrs C A, New York, Ayrault street.
Whitwell, S H, Boston, Berkeley avenue.
Wilson, Richard T, New York, Jones',Bellevue avenue.
Wheeler, Charles, Philadelphia, No. 5, Cliff Cottage.
Woolsey, Miss A H, New York, Rathbone's Washington street.
Ward, Aaron, New York, Newman's, Catherine street.
Whitehouse, J H, New York, Rutherford's, Harrison avenue.
William G M, Terre Haute, Ind, Arnold's, Rhode Island avenue.
Winslow, Surgeon George F, U S N, Hodges, Catherine street.
White, Lieut Com, Edwin,U S N, Tilton's, Mount Vernon street.
Whitwell, S H, Boston, Berkeley avenue.
Young, Frank G, Boston, Wormley's, Red Cross ave and Beach.

—••••••••—

www.ingramcontent.com/pod-product-compliance
Lightning Source LLC
Chambersburg PA
CBHW021416090426
42742CB00009B/1161